"In *Think Confident, Be Confident for Teens*, Fox and ⟨...⟩ developmental problem, low self-esteem, in a very v⟨...⟩ Using a number of case vignettes, the authors draw readers into the process to help them build a sense of personal efficacy and believe that they can do what they need to do. After following the exercises in this workbook, it would be difficult for teen readers to continue to feel badly about themselves. This is an essential book for parents, teachers, and, of course, teens."

—Arthur Freeman, Ed.D, ABPP, director of clinical psychology program at Midwestern University

"Growing as a teen means giving yourself the tools to succeed in life. This book is like your personal toolbox. Read it and carry it with you on your personal road to success."

—William Sears, MD, pediatrician and author of *The Successful Child*

"No one should travel through adolescence alone! Marci Fox and Leslie Sokol ensure this is not the case by offering *Think Confident, Be Confident for Teens*, a user-friendly coping-skills manual, as an essential companion on the journey. Fox and Sokol score with a workbook that is finely tailored to suit the needs of teenagers who are working to overcome their self-doubt, fragile self-esteem, perfectionism, painful self-consciousness, and avoidance."

—Robert D. Friedberg, PhD, ABPP, ACT, associate director of clinical training at the Pacific Graduate School of Professional Psychology at Palo Alto University

"*Think Confident, Be Confident for Teens* is an outstanding addition to the self-help literature for adolescents. Fox and Sokol have translated the powerful tools of cognitive behavioral therapy into a readable and relevant manual. Common dilemmas that teens face serve as illustrations and bring to life principles that can help young readers through a challenging and pivotal stage of development."

> —Donna M. Sudak, MD, ACT, founding fellow of the Academy of Cognitive Therapy and president of the Academy of Cognitive Therapy

"Adolescence is often characterized by severe self-doubt and worry that can create significant distress for teenagers and their families and negatively impact academic, social, and emotional functioning. Are these extreme reactions an inevitable part of the teenage transition? No! Sokol and Fox show how adolescence can be the foundation for a lifetime of self-confidence."

> —Dennis Greenberger, PhD, coauthor of *Mind Over Mood*

"Being a teen can be tough. From stresses at home or at school to problems with friends, sometimes it can feel like it's just too much. Self-doubt can creep in, leading to feelings of anxiety, worry, frustration, and sadness. There's good news, though. Based on the latest science and strategies that really work, *Think Confident, Be Confident for Teens* offers simple, useful tips that will put you on a confident path and help you see yourself in a positive, realistic light. This quick-read book can help you handle whatever comes your way."

> —Mark A. Reinecke, PhD, ABPP, ACT, professor of psychiatry and behavioral sciences at Northwestern University's Feinberg School of Medicine

"Adolescence can be a time when self-reflection and newly developed thinking styles can be a challenge. Following the lead of cognitive theory, *Think Confident, Be Confident for Teens* guides the adolescent reader though experiences and activities that will shape a healthy and more confident thinking style. A valuable resource for teens, with potential to prevent unwanted emotional turmoil."

> —Philip C. Kendall, PhD, ABPP, distinguished university professor and Laura H. Carnell Professor of Psychology at Temple University

"*Think Confident, Be Confident for Teens* is a practical, clear, and powerful guide young people can use to boost their confidence and face the inevitable obstacles of life. Filled with forms, examples, and empowering guidelines, this book will give teens the tools to take on the challenges of life."

> —Robert L. Leahy, PhD, director of the American Institute for Cognitive Therapy and author of *Beat the Blues Before They Beat You*, *The Worry Cure*, and *Anxiety Free*

"In an ideal world, *Think Confident, Be Confident for Teens* would be required reading in high school and college curricula. Speaking directly to teens on matters that concern them most, Fox and Sokol succeed in offering evidence-based ways teens can reduce their social self-consciousness, improve their outlook on themselves and their lives, and be more confident and effective in handling the sorts of stresses that teens know all too well. Adolescents suffering from that common malady known as insecurity will benefit significantly from learning the lessons taught by this valuable book."

> —Cory F. Newman, PhD, ABPP, professor of psychology in psychiatry and director of the Center for Cognitive Therapy at the University of Pennsylvania

think
confident,
be
confident
for teens

a cognitive therapy
guide to **overcoming**
self-doubt and
creating unshakable
self-esteem

MARCI G. FOX, PhD
LESLIE SOKOL, PhD

Instant Help Books
An Imprint of New Harbinger Publications, Inc.

Publisher's Note

This publication is designed to provide accurate and authoritative information in regard to the subject matter covered. It is sold with the understanding that the publisher is not engaged in rendering psychological, financial, legal, or other professional services. If expert assistance or counseling is needed, the services of a competent professional should be sought.

Distributed in Canada by Raincoast Books

Copyright © 2011 by Marci G. Fox & Leslie Sokol
New Harbinger Publications, Inc.
5674 Shattuck Avenue
Oakland, CA 94609
www.newharbinger.com

Cover design by Amy Shoup; Acquired by Tesilya Hanauer; Edited by Clancy Drake

Printed in the United States of America

Library of Congress Cataloging in Publication Data

Fox, Marci G.
  Think confident, be confident for teens : a cognitive therapy guide to overcoming self-doubt and creating unshakable self-esteem / Marci G. Fox and Leslie Sokol ; foreword by Aaron T. Beck and Judith S. Beck.
      p. cm.
  ISBN 978-1-60882-113-6 (pbk.) -- ISBN 978-1-60882-114-3 (pdf e-book) -- ISBN 978-1-60882-115-0 (epub)
  1. Self-esteem in adolescence. 2. Self-confidence in adolescence. 3. Self-perception in adolescence. 4. Teenagers--Conduct of life. I. Sokol, Leslie. II. Title.
  BF724.3.S36F69 2011
  155.5'19--dc23
                          2011027078

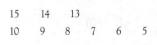

To our children, Jesse, Ethan, Carly, Chad, Alex, and Max, with love

Contents

Chapter 1

Chapter 2

Chapter 3

Foreword

Adolescence is a confusing and unsettling stage of life for many people, as they struggle to figure out who they are, what their place in the world is, and how they should relate to others. Teenagers often focus intensely on how they believe other people—especially their peers—perceive them, and they frequently err in their assessments. If their perceptions are distorted, a cognitive approach can be quite useful in helping them correct their ideas and conclusions, allowing them to see reality more clearly.

If a typical teen, for example, is excluded from a party, her immediate thought is, *My friends don't like me*. A cognitive approach can help her in several ways. One, she can look for evidence that seems to support or contradict this idea. Have her friends, or some of them at least, done other things that make her think they don't like her? Have they showed her in different ways that they do like her? Two, the teen can look to see whether there are other likely explanations for why she might have been excluded. Three, she can decatastrophize the experience by asking herself, *If it turns out they don't like me, how can I cope? What can I do?* She can also consider the best outcome of the situation as well as the most realistic outcome. Four, she can assess the impact of telling herself that her friends don't like her and the impact of changing her thinking. Five, she can reflect on the advice she would offer someone else who was in this situation and had this thought. And, six, she can do problem solving, asking herself what it would be helpful for her to do, now and in the long run.

Whether or not her initial thought is valid, this teen will feel distressed if she overgeneralizes from this one situation, because it will affect her self-esteem and self-confidence. If she believes at heart that she is a likeable person, this situation may lead her to feel temporarily annoyed, hurt, or unhappy, but it will not change her basic view of herself. On the other hand, if she doubts her likeability, she may jump from *My friends don't like me* to *No one really likes me* to *I'm unlikeable.* Cognitive techniques can help her evaluate these conclusions as well.

This book, written by our two excellent colleagues, helps teens who may continually misinterpret situations and interactions and then see themselves in unrealistically negative ways. If only all adolescents were taught to identify their thoughts (especially the thoughts about themselves) that lead to distress, to recognize that their thoughts are ideas and not necessarily truths, to evaluate their thoughts, and to respond effectively to them. There would be far less emotional angst and dysfunction in adolescents and far greater opportunities to weather the usual storms of adolescence with equanimity.

—Aaron T. Beck, MD
    president, Beck Institute for Cognitive Behavior Therapy
    university professor emeritus, University of Pennsylvania

—Judith S. Beck, PhD
    president, Beck Institute for Cognitive Behavior Therapy
    clinical associate professor of psychology in psychiatry,
    University of Pennsylvania

Acknowledgments

We owe a gigantic thank you to our terrific children. Jesse, Ethan, and Carly Fox, thank you for your unflagging support and enthusiasm. Chad, Alex, and Max Detweiler, thank you for sharing your personal stories and supplying us with a constant source of editorial help with technical language and expressions. A special thank you goes out to all of their classmates and friends from Germantown Academy who shared their struggles, insights, and innermost thoughts and feelings. Our biggest thank yous go to our amazing husbands, Stu and Bob, who held down the fort so we could devote the time to writing this book. We are so lucky to have you in our lives.

We also want to thank other family members and friends for generously lending their expertise and support, including Jodi Sokol, Liane Browne, and Doris Schwartz, for their fastidious technical editing; Marvin S. Gittes for his legal expertise; and Margaret Gittes, Stephen Schwartz, Geri and James Davis, Alvin and Esther Fox, Mark Likness, Marc Sokol, and Phyllis and Arnold Sokol. We are extremely appreciative of our brilliant colleagues Cory Newman and Emily Becker-Weidman, and thank them for their positive feedback, encouragement, and useful editorial comments. Thank you to Julie Snow Reagan and Brian Keenaghan for always being there with technical support.

We also feel so fortunate to have Anne Marie O'Farrell as our agent. Thanks for always being there, believing in us, and fighting for us. Thank you to our talented team of editors, Tesilya Hanauer, Jess Beebe, and Nicola Skidmore, for all the time, energy, and hard work you put into helping shape this book to be even better. Sincere gratitude to Clancy Drake for expertly and carefully polishing our work. You're so talented. Thanks to Leslie Davis Guccione, our teen whisperer. You are an amazing person and editor. And we could not write this or any book without recognizing our debt to the father of cognitive therapy, Aaron T. Beck, whose work has inspired so many of us.

We would like our patients and supervisees to know that they are our greatest inspiration. We greatly value what we learn from you: thank you for letting us help you grow your skills and self-confidence.

Introduction

"The greatest discovery of all time is that a person can change his future by merely changing his attitude."

—*Oprah Winfrey*

Confidence is one of the keys to success. If you have confidence, it means you believe in yourself—you know you have the brains, skills, talent, and know-how to get what you need and to handle whatever life throws at you. Unlike cockiness, which is an exaggerated view of oneself not based in reality, confidence gives you the real deal: an accurate mental picture of your strengths as well as the courage to ask for help, seek out the information you need, or acquire the skills you don't have. By learning how to generate confidence, you can unleash the incredible power of your own natural energy and, within reason, you can achieve practically anything you put your mind to.

This book will teach you how to conquer confidence's greatest opponent: doubt. Doubt—specifically self-doubt—weakens self-confidence. When you have self-doubt, you think you're in trouble when you're not, or think you can't handle things when you can. Self-doubt is the enemy in your head telling you that you fall short, that you will be rejected, or that you are a "failure." This is the same voice that tells you that you are not being the "right" kind of friend or person, or that you are not "good enough" in hobbies, sports, or academics. Self-doubt unnecessarily drains your energy and leads you away from achieving your goals, such as happiness in your personal and social life and success in your athletic endeavors, your creative pursuits, and your efforts at school and at your job, if you have one. Negative thoughts driven by self-doubt put needless obstacles in your path.

Self-doubt has a significant impact on your moods and actions, on the way you feel in your body, and on your motivation. It leads you to believe you lack intelligence, abilities, or skills even when the evidence shows otherwise. When you doubt yourself, you focus on your perceived weaknesses and don't fully consider your strengths. You unknowingly make things harder on yourself. You get in your own way.

There's good news. Self-doubt can be defeated. In this book we'll teach you how to get off the path of doubt and walk firmly on the path of confidence. With confidence, you'll feel better about yourself and experience all the rewards that go with these positive feelings. We'll show you how to retrain your brain based on the principles of cognitive therapy. Through this new system of thinking, you will develop and strengthen what we call your confidence mindset.

A *confidence mindset* allows you to have both the most positive *and* the most accurate view of yourself and any given situation. Giving yourself the credit you have earned and going after what you want are signs of confidence. When you acknowledge your shortcomings and appreciate your strengths, you can free yourself from doubt and insecurity and your confidence will soar.

Our program helps you weaken and eventually erase the opposite of the confidence mindset: the *self-doubt mindset*, which involves seeing yourself in a negatively biased and inaccurate way. We'll show you how to put yourself on an even playing field with everyone else so that you stop ignoring or minimizing your assets and strengths, second-guessing and criticizing yourself, and getting paralyzed when you're trying to come up with a plan of action or a decision.

How Cognitive Therapy Concepts Can Help

Cognitive therapy is based on this basic rule: how we think influences how we feel, how we behave, and even how our bodies react to our circumstances. In other words, situations don't make you feel or respond in a certain way. It's how you interpret each situation that affects how you feel or respond. Thus, a situation may *feel* upsetting, but it's actually your thoughts about the situation that drive your distress. So if you want to change your reaction, start with your thinking.

Suppose, for example, that it's the end of summer with two weeks left until school starts. You want to get in shape so you won't suffer on the athletic field; or maybe it's time to tackle your required reading before there's no time left. But you may find that shifting your behavior requires a change in thinking.

Your thoughts can interfere with your ability to take action. You may have thoughts that give you permission to put things off, such as "It can wait; I still have plenty of time; I want to enjoy every minute left of my summer, because once school starts it's going to be torture." These types of thoughts can lead you away from your goals and toward trouble.

Changing the way you think can alter the way you act. Imagine thinking, "I can get on top of things by starting today. I can't wait around to want to. Starting now will be a warm-up and will make returning to the athletic field so much easier. I might even get ahead and be able to wind up with a few days of fun or chilling out before school starts rather than scrambling at the last second." Thoughts are powerful tools that play a major role in whether we take action or not, and they determine what action we take.

The doubt-driven thoughts that interfere with appropriate or effective action are what we call *give-up thoughts*. We define give-up thoughts as biased perceptions of the truth. They often reflect how you feel rather than the factual reality of any given situation. You can learn to identify these give-up thoughts and, instead of blindly accepting them as true, you can learn to carefully examine their validity. We'll teach you to replace give-up thoughts with *go-to thoughts*. Go-to thoughts are accurate, clear, and unbiased perceptions of any given situation, and they are always more helpful than give-up thoughts. Go-to thoughts are essential tools for a happy, successful life.

Sometimes when your thinking gets you into trouble, it is because you are looking at the world through a clouded lens—what we call a *doubt distortion*. Doubt distortions are ways in which you unknowingly filter information in a negative way to fit a negative way that you feel. Instead of seeing the facts, you believe the distortion—and the distortion is untrue. For instance, you may believe that someone is not interested in you when there is no information to support that thought, or there is information to the contrary. You simply cannot see and believe in the facts because your feelings—of fear or self-doubt, for example—are so strong they cloud your judgment.

These sorts of distorted views tend to be worse when we're stressed out or upset. Stress can be divided into two kinds: genuine and artificial. *Genuine stress* happens when a real, difficult situation shows up in your life. An example might be if your car gets a flat tire when you are rushing to an important event, or if you find out at the last minute that you have a test you did not know about.

In contrast, *artificial stress* happens when we create a stressful situation in our own minds. For example, you may push yourself to finish a paper two weeks ahead of time to give yourself a lot of time to proofread it, or you may become overly concerned about what your hair looks like when you're headed to the gym. Placing unrealistic or overly harsh demands on yourself can lead to stress just as surely as having to deal with something hard that happens to you.

Stress, whether genuine or artificial, becomes stronger when we think we can't handle the difficulty. When stress gets the best of us, our insecurities come to the surface, and self-doubt can take over our thoughts, leading us to be unreasonably hard on ourselves. This happens to all of us from time to time. Self-doubt makes us assume the person we like won't like us back, that we won't be invited to the party, or that we won't do well on a test, get the part, or make the team.

The tools of cognitive therapy that you'll learn in this book will teach you to identify self-doubt and transform it into confidence—to replace give-up thoughts with go-to thoughts. One of the simplest ways to begin changing your thinking is to remember that thoughts aren't always true. Have you ever seen that bumper sticker "Don't believe everything you think"? Well, it is true that you can't always trust or believe your own self-doubting thoughts. When you learn to identify your own self-doubts and understand the types of thinking that are getting you in trouble, you can replace these self-doubting thoughts with confidence-boosting thoughts that actually help you reach your goals.

How to Use This Book

In the first three chapters, we'll act as your personal confidence building coaches, helping you retrain your brain to move from doubt to confidence. Chapter 1 will show you how to identify doubt and understand how it operates and interferes with confidence. Chapter 2 is designed to help you begin to really notice your thinking and develop a more accurate view of yourself and the world around you. In chapter 3, you will learn to take action to build greater self-confidence.

Then, in chapters 4 through 7, you'll find stories from other teens about typical situations that stress them out. The teen stories in these chapters will give you an opportunity to learn from other teens' experiences. Reading them, you'll become familiar with "give-up" or self-doubt thoughts that can sabotage you. Then you'll learn alternative ways of thinking about the situation to free you from self-doubt and allow you to consider the path of self-confidence. You'll see how to replace your give-up thoughts with confident go-to thoughts. Finally, you will use what you've learned to develop a confidence mindset—the ability to see yourself and situations in a positive, accurate, and realistic way—that you can call on at any time, in any situation.

We encourage you to read the stories even if they're not about issues you're struggling with. It doesn't actually matter if the give-up thoughts aren't the same as yours: they will still help you learn to recognize and replace give-up thoughts with confident go-to thoughts. For instance, even though it wouldn't matter to you that your friend didn't pick you as a lab partner, another person might think, *I wasn't smart enough. My friend is not the friend I think he is. My friend thinks he'd get a better grade without me.* You can see how a person's thinking can generate a lot of distress. In this case, maybe the facts really are that the friend simply asked the person sitting next to him and didn't think anything of it, or maybe the friend didn't have the chance to ask this person because his neighbor asked him first. Seeing how these sorts of mistaken thoughts and behaviors get started, you may be able to better understand a situation that you're struggling with.

Finally, chapter 8 guides you to grow unshakable self-confidence through exercises designed to assess, repair, grow, and maintain your confidence. At the same time, we review specific strategies you can use to stop doubt from getting in your way.

Let Us Know How You're Doing

It can be helpful to share your successes and struggles with others. Let others know how this book has helped you. Let us know which strategies have made a difference for you. Join our blog at thinkconfidentteens.blogspot.com or e-mail us at info@thinkconfidentbeconfident.com. That way you can hear from us and from other teens as well.

CHAPTER 1

What's Going On?
Understanding Self-Doubt and
the Confidence Mindset

*"If you don't have confidence, you'll
always find a way not to win."*

—Carl Lewis (multisport Olympian)

Have you ever felt down about yourself? Self-critical? Lacking in confidence? Uncertain or insecure? Then you've felt self-doubt. We all feel self-doubt sometimes. You may not be aware of it because you haven't labeled it as such before. Self-doubt impacts how we think, how we feel, and how we act. It gets expressed in lots of different ways.

For example, consider Meghan, a girl in her first year at college. She wants to try out for the field hockey team. She held her own on her high school team—and she knows it—and she loved the camaraderie she felt on the team. She'd hoped she would get to play in college, but now that she's competing against the top girls for a few spots, she's not sure she can do it.

Instead of heading to the try-outs thinking she has what it takes and that she just needs the opportunity to show it, she is full of self-doubt. It shows up in her body: her stomach is queasy, her muscles feel tight, and her legs feel shaky. It dominates her feelings: usually outgoing and comfortable in her own skin, she feels shy, awkward, worried, and even a little ashamed as she steps out on the field for try-outs. It poisons her thoughts: her mind works double-time to convince her that the situation is unwinnable, that she doesn't measure up, that she'd be happier doing something else—anything else. Her self-doubt makes her very uncomfortable, even miserable, and it saps her ability to do her best at the try-outs—or even to show up for them at all.

Or consider Joe, a sophomore in high school who denies he has self-doubt. He says, "My group is really tight." Yet when his friends make plans for the weekend, he often feels anxious, lonely, and left out. He wants to have friends over but thinks, *Why would they want to hang out here?* When Joe does hang out with his friends, he rarely takes an active role in making plans and just follows along with the crowd. He holds back because he secretly fears his friends won't think he's cool. He hasn't put a name to it, but it's his self-doubt that makes him question whether people like him, making him watchful and worried instead of being able to just let go and have a good time with people *he* likes—his friends.

Stress can intensify feelings of self-doubt until you feel overwhelmed by self-criticism, second-guessing, and negative thoughts about many aspects of your life. Stress-fueled self-doubt can lead you to feel afraid, anxious, sad, and irritable. It can cause you to respond to situations more intensely than you need to, and to draw conclusions that don't really add up—for example, thinking either that your teacher doesn't like you or that you'll get a bad grade because the teacher yelled at you for talking in class.

How Self-Doubt Can Affect You

Self-doubt can lie dormant for long periods. It can operate quietly, slowly and systematically affecting your whole identity in a negative way. It may also suddenly attack and destroy the factually based realistic and positive thoughts you have about yourself. Self-doubt:

- skews past, current, and future information;

- colors in a negative way how you think, feel, and act;

- causes you to feel uncertain or insecure about how to face or respond to a situation;

- bombards you with self-criticism, second-guessing, and negative thoughts;

- causes you to take the blame for things, even when you know you've done nothing wrong;

- leads you into fear, anxiety, sadness, or irritability;

- causes your emotional reactions to be way out of proportion to the situations you find yourself in.

Where Self-Doubt Comes From

Self-doubt arises from our genetic makeup as well as our life experiences, the messages we hear, and our social interactions. Your own temperament has been part of you since birth. Did your parents or other adults ever tell you what you were like as a baby? For example:

- Were you a baby who slept through everything? (And are you still a deep sleeper?)

- Were you an easily startled baby? (And are you still awakened by the slightest disturbance?)

- Were you a baby who had to be held all the time?

- Were you a baby who sat contentedly in your stroller entertaining yourself?

- Were you a baby your parents could take anywhere?

- Were you a baby who was always screaming, or described as "difficult"?

Your answers to these questions are clues to your temperament. Babies who cling and cry are normal; babies who are mellow and calm are normal: they simply have different temperaments.

Think about how you react to situations now. What are you like? Do you consider yourself easygoing, or overreactive? These are ways to describe and understand your temperament, and they are a part of the definition of who you are. For example:

- Are you one of those people who jumps out of bed in the morning full of energy and crashes at night?

- Are you the type who wakes up, moves in slow motion until fully awake, and then needs to wind down before you get to sleep?

- Do you let people know how you are feeling?

- Do you keep your feelings to yourself?

- Do you like being around a lot of people?

- Do you prefer to be alone, or with a few close friends?

- Are you the eternal optimist always trying to make the best of any situation?

- Are you the perpetual pessimist always seeing the worst in every situation?

Your answers to these questions tell you something about how you're wired: how you express yourself and your social and individual nature.

Now think about grade school. If you had to leave the classroom for extra help (in reading, say), what were your thoughts and feelings? Were you upset because you were being separated from your friends? Were you okay with being pulled out of class because you had friends who were also getting extra reading help? Were you distressed because getting extra reading help made you feel stupid? What about if you were the last one picked for the team on the playground? Did you think it was because someone didn't like you? Did you think it was because you weren't good enough?

How you react to life situations tells you important information about how you define yourself. Your yes or no answers above paint a picture of who you are: tightly wound or relaxed, fiery or slow burning, a social butterfly or an independent, an optimist or a pessimist. Who you are plays a role in how situations affect you. Although all situations have the potential to generate doubt, most often it is not really the situation itself that upsets you but your interpretation of what happened. In the situations given above, needing extra reading help or not being picked for a team is a problem only when you allow it to mean something negative about you. When situations lead you to draw personal, negative conclusions about yourself, then you know your self-doubt has been activated. Your answers tell you where your doubt lies, whether it is doubt about your ability to perform or concern about being liked.

Clearly, if you experienced a lot of difficulties while growing up, you are more likely to experience self-doubt—though not everyone's self-confidence is compromised by difficult life events. Here are some examples of life experiences—some very serious and even tragic, others less so but still important—that can plant the seeds of self-doubt, or make them grow:

- Conflict or even violence in your home

- Parents separating or getting divorced

- Significant illness or injury—either your own or that of a family member or friend

- Death of a family member or friend

- Transferring to a new school or moving to a new area

- Perceived favoritism of you or a sibling

- Difficulties with your siblings

- Not making the team

- Auditioning for a part in a play or a place in a musical group and not getting it

- Having no one to sit with at lunch; feeling like you don't fit in anywhere

- Being bullied or teased

- Not being invited to parties or included by your peers; not having as many social plans as your peers

- Struggling with schoolwork; getting poor grades

- Being placed in a lower track in school

- Being considerably poorer financially than your peers

- Being different in any way from most others in your school or neighborhood (height, weight, race, sexual orientation)

As an exercise, make a list of important events or situations that may have shaped your self-doubt: a parent who traveled for work or who couldn't find work; moving to a different town or school; divorced parents; remarried parents; a sick sibling; a bad sports injury—the possibilities are endless, and will be different for everyone. Just one or two important events can plant the seed of self-doubt; later events provide the fertilizer for it to grow.

As you think of the events of your life, consider how you view them. Because much of the time it is not the event itself that upsets you: it is your interpretation of it. You can grow up in a relatively safe and secure home and still be filled with self-doubt. Or you can experience many disadvantages or setbacks and still have a good share of self-worth. How you make sense of your experiences plays a role in whether or not you develop a sense of self-doubt because of them.

For example, not being invited to a particular party might cause one person to think she wasn't liked, while another might think she wasn't good enough, and another person would not take it personally at all. While one person might think his parents' divorce is his fault, another might recognize that the divorce has to do with her parents' relationship and not with anything she may or may not have done.

What Do You Value?

When you recognize that you matter and have something valuable to contribute to the world, then you have a sense of self-worth. Your self-worth is directly connected to what you care deeply about. Do you see yourself as possessing qualities you deem most important, such as being smart or loyal? If so, you have a strong sense of self-worth. Or do you believe you fall short of possessing certain important qualities? If so, then self-doubt is dominating your view of the world.

Many people gain their sense of self-worth in two main ways: through achievement or through social interactions and relationships. What makes you feel good about yourself is directly connected to which of these you value more. Do you care most about accomplishments and getting things done, such as getting good grades or performing well at sports? Then you are more *achievement oriented*. Or do you care more about your relationships and taking care of others, such as being a reliable friend, being liked, and being a good person? Then you are more *socially oriented*. Or you may be a mix of the two.

For example, if there were a sign-up sheet for an off-campus day, would you: a) sign up for what you think might look good on your resume; b) poll your friends before you sign your name to anything, paying less attention to what you'd prefer; or c) try to talk your friends into making a group plan to do what might look best on your college application or be the activity you would prefer?

Are You Achievement Oriented?

_____ I set goals and strive to reach them.

_____ My self-worth comes from my performance in school, athletics, extracurricular activities, or doing what I want to do.

_____ If I have to choose between doing what I want to do or an opportunity to be social, I typically choose what I want to do.

_____ I prefer to be considered capable or smart rather than nice or friendly.

_____ I take my social life for granted and place more importance on working hard to succeed or on doing what I want.

_____ I define myself by what I do and not by how much people like me.

_____ I like competition.

_____ I perform better when I am competing.

_____ I enjoy doing what I like even if no one wants to do it with me.

Are You Socially Oriented?

_____ I feel that being loved or accepted is better than accomplishing a task.

_____ I believe it's more important to be viewed as nice than smart.

_____ I care about what other people think of me.

_____ I tend to pick what others want to do over what I want to do.

_____ It's more important to me to be liked than to do what seems right for me.

_____ I find it easier to go with the flow than to step on anyone's toes.

_____ I don't like competition and am likely to fall apart under pressure to compete.

_____ I am more likely to be concerned about what others think when I choose my clothes, cut my hair, or act silly.

_____ My goals are easily swayed by the influence of others.

_____ My self-worth comes from my social success.

_____ I'd rather be with my friends than do any given activity.

Your answers to these questions can give you a general idea of what drives you: achievement, social connection, or both. The achievement-oriented person takes pride in personal accomplishments. He or she focuses on getting things done and values independence, freedom, and mobility. A connection-focused person cares most about being a good person and being valued by others. Friendship and the needs, feelings, and opinions of others matter the most. People who place high value on both achievement and relationships are driven to achieve in both areas.

What Bothers You?

If you care deeply about something, you may place greater value on your ability to succeed in that area of concern. The internal pressure you place on yourself to achieve or do well socially is normal and useful, but when you doubt your ability to succeed in areas that are important to you, your self-worth suffers. Situations are uniquely stressful for each of us based on whether or not they activate our doubt. It's not the pressure to perform that creates your stress. Rather, it's the self-doubt that you have about whether you can deliver that bothers you. Doubt causes you to see positive, neutral, and even genuinely negative experiences more negatively and as a reflection of your own shortcomings. When you see situations and your strengths more objectively, you are less likely to have doubt as the source of your distress. Whether you care about achievement, social relationships, or both will affect what situations bother you.

It is common to take for granted your strength in one area while feeling vulnerable in another. If you place high value on achievement, then anything that interferes with your ability to achieve is likely to activate your insecurity, while social challenges may be of a lesser concern. In contrast, if you place greater value on the social goals of being liked or being a good person, then real or imagined interpersonal conflict or rejection will more likely activate your insecurity, while not performing well at any given task may be less distressing. When you put high values on both achieving and being liked, your self-worth is likely to be more fragile, since trouble in either area may result in self-doubt.

What Bothers Achievement-Oriented People Most?

- criticism, whether real or imagined
- feeling as though you have no control
- loss of independence; a feeling of being smothered
- difficulty achieving a goal
- being told to do something, not asked
- not living up to your own expectations

What Bothers Socially Oriented People Most?

- rejection, whether real or imagined
- disagreement with another person
- being left out or not included
- having someone upset with you
- a sense of awkwardness in a social situation
- not being called or texted back
- someone judging your character

The Voice of Self-Doubt

When your ability to achieve or to experience what you value is compromised, your self-doubt tends to rise to the surface and cloud your perspective.

Instead of seeing yourself in an accurate way, you may call yourself nasty names: these names have everything to do with self-doubt and nothing to do with who you really are.

Here are some typical names achievement-focused people call themselves when things don't go as planned, are difficult, or turn out badly: failure, loser, inept, incompetent, dumb, stupid, incapable, inferior, weak, pathetic, gutless, lazy, not good enough, don't measure up. Here are some typical names people focused on social relationships call themselves when they feel rejected, left out, or judged: unattractive, unlikeable, bad, unlovable, unworthy, ugly, reject, nerd, loser, weirdo, defect, flawed, drip, bore, geek, socially awkward.

Does one or more of these names match the name or names you call yourself? If not, can you name your personal self-doubting insult?

I am (a) _____.

(We'll do an exercise in chapter 2 that challenges this doubt-based belief.)

Teens who let their self-doubt be in charge often see a situation as more challenging than it really is, and they can opt out before they even try. For example, self-doubt is talking when you fear asking someone to be your lab partner, even though the odds are they will say yes; or when you don't try out for the part in the play because you think you won't get the role. These thoughts—the kind that urge you to stop before you begin—are what we call give-up thoughts.

Give-Up Thoughts

Self-doubt expresses itself through give-up thoughts. These thoughts get us off track or into trouble; they paralyze us or cause us to move in the opposite direction of our goals, needs, or desires. Give-up thoughts are usually subjective, inaccurate, biased ways of interpreting a situation. Even if there is only a tiny kernel of truth in the thought, the thought is blown out of proportion so that it leaves you unable to move forward, problem solve, or feel good. Instead of accepting and allowing these give-up thoughts to govern how you feel and behave, you can learn to recognize them. You can learn to question their validity and break their power over you.

Give-up thoughts are self-critical. They are driven by insecurity and uncertainty and lead to second-guessing yourself. If no one has trained you to pay attention to these thoughts, they often go by unnoticed, and you can blindly accept them even if they are not true. Here are some examples of situations that might lead you to give-up thoughts if you lack self-confidence:

Situation	Give-Up Thought
Your boyfriend breaks up with you.	I knew it was too good to be true; he never really liked me and was just using me. I blew my only chance. This stinks; it's going to mess up my whole year.
You bomb a test.	It's pointless to try now; it's already too late. I don't have what it takes, who am I kidding? This material is just too hard. No one gets this stuff—why bother?
You get in trouble.	It's too late now; I give up. There's something wrong with me that I'm always getting in trouble. I'm bad.
Your friends leave you out of their plans.	I guess I'm low on the list. Maybe there's something wrong with me. I'm just not fun to be with. Maybe I don't really have any friends.

Warning

Give-up thoughts mess you up and won't help you get you where you want to go.

Getting Off the Self-Doubt Path

Not every thought that pops into our heads is a statement of truth. Sometimes our thoughts are accurate reflections of fact, and at other times they are biased reflections of our insecurity or doubt. It's important to learn how to recognize when your thoughts are valid and when they are not. When thoughts are not valid, distortions of truth, or unhelpful in that they keep us from our goals, they are doubt-driven give-up thoughts. You have the power to stop walking down the self-doubt path; all it takes is a more analytical perspective.

We'll teach you that perspective here. School, too, is teaching you to think critically. You have likely learned to examine hypotheses by researching in the library and the lab. You have used measurable observations to identify the factual results of your experiments, and then you have used logic to draw conclusions based on those facts. Applying these principles to your self-doubt-based give-up thoughts will allow you to get off the path of self-doubt. Self-doubt is the negative, subjective interpretation or conclusion you draw about yourself, which is often based on feelings rather than facts. Self-doubt causes you to believe distressing situations mean something negative or deficient about you. You can counter it by:

◆ collecting data;

◆ examining it; and

◆ drawing new conclusions based solely on the facts.

As a critical thinker, you can use the facts to see the world accurately and clearly—even when you're trying to understand something very close to you that you have strong feelings about. Learning to see the facts takes practice. It's easier to let your feelings get the best of you and talk you into believing something that isn't necessarily true. Looking carefully at the facts takes effort. You must:

◆ look at situations from more than one perspective;

◆ stay open to lots of options;

- think things through; and

- be willing to change your mind.

Go-To Thoughts

Go-to thoughts are the most reasonable, reliable, accurate, fact-based, unbiased conclusions that you can draw about a particular situation. These thoughts come from an analysis of the situation that allows you to see the truth. Go-to thoughts provide a different way of looking at the same situation. They enable you to see the big picture of who you are rather than focusing on any single (perceived) shortcoming.

Now let's take a second look at the typical life situations listed in the previous table and replace the give-up thoughts with go-to thoughts:

Situation	Give-Up Thoughts	Go-To Thoughts
Your boyfriend breaks up with you.	I knew it was too good to be true; he never really liked me and was just using me.	He told me he liked me, he acted like he liked me, and he told other people he liked me. Just because he wants to break up doesn't mean he never liked me. Regardless of how he feels now, what we had was real.
	I blew my only chance.	It feels like this was my only chance, but given how many boys are out there, I have every reason to think I will have relationships in the future.
	This stinks; it's going to mess up my whole year.	I have the power to let this mess up my year or to put it in perspective, knowing my sadness is temporary and getting busy doing what I like.

Using an analytical perspective, you start with the facts ("He told me he liked me, he acted like he liked me, and he told other people he liked me"; "There are a lot of other boys out there"), which show you that your give-up thoughts were not truthful statements about this actually distressing situation. Then, instead of doubt making you assume the worst is ahead, the facts can help you see the realistic probabilities ("I have every reason to think I will have relationships in the future"; "My sadness is temporary").

Here are a few more examples of using facts and analysis to convert give-up thoughts to go-to thoughts:

Situation	Give-Up Thoughts	Go-To Thoughts
You bomb a test.	It's pointless to try now; it's already too late.	It's one test, and it's worth only a small percentage of my grade.
	I don't have what it takes; who am I kidding?	I won't know if I have what it takes to do well if I quit before I try. I can read, think, retain information, and problem solve, so there is no reason to think I can't get this.
	This material is just too hard. No one gets this stuff, so why bother?	The material is hard, but I can ask for extra help. Just because it's hard doesn't mean I can't learn it.

Situation	Give-Up Thoughts	Go-To Thoughts
You get in trouble.	It's too late now; I give up. There's something wrong with me that I'm always getting in trouble. I'm just bad.	It's too late only if I give up. There is always a chance I can improve my situation if I try. Just because I messed up doesn't mean there's something wrong with me but it does suggest that I'm not doing what I'm supposed to be doing. I have the power to change that by playing by the rules. There are lots of times that I do well and don't get in trouble, and that defines me as well. So it's not true that I am "just bad."
Your friends leave you out of their plans.	I guess I'm low on the list. Maybe there's something wrong with me. I'm just not fun to be with. Maybe I don't really have any friends.	Just because they didn't include me tonight doesn't necessarily mean I'm low on the list. There could be all sorts of explanations. I know my friend's dad is really strict on how many people he can take in his car. Or maybe they just thought I didn't want to go. It's not reasonable to jump to the conclusion that something is wrong with me if I'm not on the list tonight. My friends always laugh when I joke around. The reality is that I have friends. There are times when I can't or don't include all my friends. It doesn't mean anything about the friendship. Not everyone can be included all the time. I don't have to make this one time mean anything it doesn't.

In each of these cases, instead of assuming the worst possible outcome, you can consider the realistic possibilities. Instead of making broad, sweeping, negative conclusions about yourself, you can put the event into perspective and move forward with your life.

Staying on the Confidence Path

When you are armed with go-to thoughts, it is much easier to stay on the confidence path—the path that leads to constructive action and wise choices, that lets you reach your goals and get what you want and need without negative consequences. It frees you to choose your own course. The confidence path allows you to:

◆ do things that you believe are important, even if you are afraid to;

◆ take appropriate risks;

◆ head toward realistic goals;

◆ minimize procrastination;

◆ plan;

◆ assert yourself;

◆ go places alone without fear or embarrassment;

◆ say no when you need or want to;

◆ try new things;

◆ problem solve and make thoughtful decisions.

All these behaviors and abilities reinforce a confidence mindset. If you are to succeed in life, it is essential that your confidence mindset take root and grow. You can provide the fertilizer and nutrients to grow it faster and stronger by practicing testing your thoughts for accuracy and by choosing to think realistically and confidently. Doing this cements the confident conclusions in your brain, and they become more and more habitual. You can also support your confidence by listening to confidence-building songs; sending yourself confidence-boosting texts; or writing confident statements on your wall on Facebook. The confidence mindset is your own personal cheerleader, coach, and friend giving you great advice. Learn to listen to it so you can permanently weed out self-doubt and grow self-confidence. Life will be easier and a lot more enjoyable!

The Bottom Line

Self-doubt negatively impacts your moods, your actions, the way you feel in your body, and your motivation. Doubt leads you to beat yourself up through self-criticism, second-guessing, and focusing on your perceived shortcomings when you buy into your give-up thoughts and feelings without checking them out to see if they're true. By understanding and labeling your self-doubt and knowing where it comes from, you are more aware of what situations may make you feel more vulnerable, and you'll be able to identify when your thinking comes more from self-doubt than from the facts of each situation.

Self-confidence is believing in yourself because you are able to see yourself in a positive, accurate, and realistic way. When your thoughts are accurate, you know you have the skills or resources to handle whatever comes your way. We all get hit at times with negative situations, and sometimes our concerns are valid and require a course of action. It's when we attach a negative personal meaning to a positive, neutral, or negative event that self-doubt takes over. Confidence comes from seeing situations objectively. Learning to focus on the facts will enable you to replace your biased give-up thoughts with unbiased, objective go-to thoughts. By growing your confidence mindset you can see all that life has to offer and go for it.

CHAPTER 2

What Are You Thinking? Capturing and Analyzing the Thoughts That Bring You Down

"Sometimes in life you don't always feel like a winner, but that doesn't mean you're not a winner."

—Lady Gaga

Thoughts have great power, and they provide the fuel for both doubt and confidence. What gets us into trouble is how we *think* about situations and not the situation per se. Identifying biased, inaccurate thoughts and replacing them with valid, truthful alternatives is a key to well-being and success. Simply put, situations don't cause you to feel a certain way. It's your perception or interpretation—your thinking—that influences how you feel and behave and the bodily sensations you experience.

We all have thoughts that pop into our head (positive, neutral, and negative). Positive, encouraging thoughts help build self-confidence while neutral thoughts have nothing to do with an evaluation of the self and don't affect us. It is the negatively biased thoughts that cause us distress. Our thoughts are sometimes partial expressions of true fact—or even completely true reflections of fact—but our thoughts can also be distortions of truth, or they can be entirely false. Thoughts that are inaccurate, or are distortions of truth, can play havoc on your mood, cause your body to overreact, and lead you to ineffective behavior. In this chapter we will train you to think about your thinking. When you pay attention to shifts in your mood or in your body, you can use these as a signal that it's time to check in with yourself. Think about a warning signal that goes off on your mobile phone. It could be an alert to charge the battery or empty your mailbox, a sign of serious malfunction, or just a temporary glitch in your operating system that disappears on its own. You can think about the thoughts that pop into your head in the same way. Sometimes they are valid and are reason for concern; and sometimes they are not valid, and they create alarm that is unnecessary and unwarranted.

Capturing Your Thoughts

You can learn to pay attention to what you think. The first step in examining your thinking is capturing your thoughts. What's going on in your head? It could be a thought. It could be the meaning you attach to that thought—or to a memory, the time of year, a dream, and so on. It could be a picture, and the thoughts and meanings you attach to it.

EXERCISE: Capture Your Thoughts

Here are two typical situations you might face. What might you think in each situation?

1. Imagine walking into your new homeroom/advisory and none of your friends are in your room. Does something like this go through your mind?

- *Another boring year—I got the worst homeroom/advisory.*

- *This stinks.*

- *This will give me the chance to get to know other people.*

- *At least I got a really good teacher.*

- You picture yourself miserable with no one to talk to.

  Or do you have a thought or picture that's completely different from these?

2. Now imagine your teacher has just told you an important test is going to be a take-home exam. Does something like this go through your mind?

- *Yes! Now I can get a good grade.*

- *This is going to be easy.*

- *I studied for no reason.*

- *Now the test is going to be so much longer.*

- You picture yourself spending hours glued to your book.

  Or do you have a thought or picture that's completely different from these?

You can also learn to look at your emotions to see if your thinking is impacting you in a negative way. When feelings are intense, they are usually linked to thoughts. Use your feelings as a warning signal that it's time to collect your thoughts: When you feel sad, angry, irritated, anxious, frustrated, insecure, disappointed, annoyed, ashamed, embarrassed, panicked, fearful, distressed, lonely, hurt, rejected, angry, guilty, or any other unpleasant emotion, ask yourself what you are thinking. Likewise, when your emotional response is way out of proportion to the situation, ask yourself what you are thinking.

Intense bodily symptoms or sensations can also be signs to pay attention to your thinking. When you notice your body responding to a situation, the response is usually connected to thoughts. Bodily cues can include tears, trembling, chest discomfort, jitteriness, butterflies, sweating, restlessness, or breathlessness, to name a few. Think of those reactions as additional warning signals that it's time to pay attention to your thoughts.

Start by Calming Yourself

When our emotions or bodily sensations are extreme, it's hard to capture our thoughts—even though that's the time when we most need to understand our thinking. The more relaxed we are, the easier the access to our thoughts, so strategies that make us calm can help us collect our thoughts more easily. Here are some to practice:

- Close your mouth and take a few slow breaths in and out of your nose.

- Make a fist and hold it, feeling the tension in your hand. Then blow air into your hand as you release the tension and open your fist.

- Whistle or hum a tune.

- Listen to some of your favorite songs.

- Close your eyes and count backwards from ten.

- Think of your favorite place or time and put yourself back there. Try to use memories formed by all five senses to make the image in your mind more vivid.

- Call a friend and talk about something else.

- Take a walk or do some exercise.

- Answer e-mails or texts.

- Tackle a task.

◆ Focus on your surroundings. Ask yourself what you see, hear, smell, feel, or taste, or describe something to yourself in as much detail as possible.

◆ Leaf through a magazine.

◆ Look at photos.

◆ Play a video or computer game.

◆ Take a bath or shower or go for a swim.

◆ Make something: bake a cake or do a craft.

When you're calm enough to see your thoughts clearly, it's time to see if your thoughts are based on realistic concern or on self-doubt.

Keys to Capturing Your Thoughts

◆ Ask yourself what you're thinking.

◆ Note strong feelings or bodily sensations and use them as warning signals and cues to pay attention to your thinking.

Ask Whether You're Experiencing Realistic Concern, or Self-Doubt

We all have an internal alarm system inside of us that prompts us toward action in difficult situations. For example, your internal alarm stops you in your tracks when a car honks as you step off the curb. Your alarmed body cues you to take appropriate action and jump out of harm's way. Or imagine you have a math test tomorrow and you forgot your notes and math book at school. If you had planned to study and absolutely need them, then concern is appropriate. Hurrying to contact the smart guy in your class is a wise strategy. When your alarm system goes off because you have a *realistic concern*, this means you sense a genuinely challenging or dangerous situation and need to take action to face the threat. Realistic concern happens when your apprehensive thoughts are valid and appropriate. Here are some more examples:

- You have a paper to write, you waited until the last minute, and now recognize you have allotted too little time to complete it.

- Your best friend has been in an accident and was rushed to the hospital.

- You are doing something you know you shouldn't—something you wouldn't want your parents, teachers, coaches, or school to find out about.

- You know you are breaking rules or the law.

- You are doing something that you know could potentially hurt you or someone else.

Self-doubt, on the other hand, leads you to think you're in trouble, will be rejected, can't handle a situation, or won't make the cut, without any real data to back those thoughts up. Your internal alarm goes off before you have actually faced the situation, and you imagine the worst outcome, seeing danger where it doesn't exist. Your imagination becomes more dangerous than the facts of the real world. You believe your thoughts and feelings are true simply because you think or feel them—even though there are no objective facts to support them. For example:

- You see failure before it has happened.

- You think your friend won't want to hang out with you before you have even asked.

- You're convinced of a negative outcome even when the reality that has presented itself is positive.

◆ You fail to believe you did a good job even when you have already received positive feedback.

◆ You think people don't want to hang out with you even when they physically are already with you.

When you give in to doubt, you cease to believe you can.

Don't Let Emotions Take Over

Aside from physical signs, there are other ways to determine if your reaction to a situation is realistic or if it is based on doubt. One has to do with time: ask yourself if the situation is happening right now, and not in the past or future. Realistic concern often has to do with a present-moment situation and with thoughts that are true and based on the facts of the situation; doubt usually has to do with imagining the future or obsessing about the past.

Another clue that your concern may be based in doubt and not reality is that you are feeling so emotional that it's hard to think straight. Emotions can rise to the point of becoming uncomfortable and clouding your ability to see the truth; when they do, they fuel your doubt. Here are signs that your emotions are getting the best of you in a given situation:

◆ Your thinking is based mostly or entirely on your feelings. (*I feel bad, therefore something bad happened, is happening, or is about to happen.*)

◆ You focus on your feelings more than on the facts. (*I feel bad, therefore this situation must be much worse than it appears to be.*)

◆ You let your feelings make your decisions. (*This situation feels so bad, I can't stand to think it through rationally. I'll go do something that helps me forget all this.*)

Feelings are an essential part of being human. They connect us to other people and allow for an emotionally satisfying life. Paying too much attention to your negative or fearful emotions, however, can cause you unnecessary distress. Focusing on them can make them more intense, severe, and frequent. Acknowledge your feelings and appreciate them them, but don't give them so much attention that you lose sight of other important things.

Your emotions deserve attention and give you important pieces of information. However, they can also sometimes be an unreliable, inaccurate source of information. You may feel a certain way, but that does not mean those feelings are reflections of truth. You may feel sad and conclude that your friend is mad at you when her behavior simply reflects that she's having a bad day or is feeling under the weather. You may feel dejected and decide that you did poorly in an interview when you did just fine. Instead of relying solely on your emotions, use other sources of information too. Don't let your feelings bully you into thinking things that are not supported by facts. Facts are your best resource.

Look at the Facts

Your distorted responses–your give-up thoughts—are judgments, biased perceptions, subjective feelings and not representations of truth; they are reflections of doubt. Doubt distorted perceptions lead to negative inaccurate conclusions. These give-up thoughts keep you from looking at situations objectively and guide you toward problematic choices. Instead of blindly accepting these thoughts and letting them get in your way, accept that just thinking something doesn't mean it's true. Recognizing this helps you see situations through a clear, unbiased lens and examine your thoughts in detail.

Just like in a courtroom, rarely is one piece of evidence enough to make a case. Piles of data are needed to convince a jury, and similarly plenty of data may be necessary for you to see the complete, accurate picture. Here's how to get and use the data you need:

1. Collect the facts, getting information from more than one source.

2. Consider all the possibilities, looking at the facts from different angles.

3. Consider your past experiences.

4. Be careful not to jump to conclusions or make broad generalizations.

Collect the Facts, Getting Information from More than One Source

Facts represent evidence-based reality. They cannot be argued with. Ask yourself, "What is the proof?" and you will be collecting facts. Facts are (for example): the try-outs for the team are Tuesday at three; people in your grade level are eligible to play for the team; you can make the scheduled practice times; you know the rules of the game and have experience playing it. Use facts as your basis, and reject any other information you get that contradicts your facts.

Accurate information can't always be found from a single source. [Facts alone will not always tell you everything you need to know, and sometimes you don't have many facts to work with. You can use other kinds of information to create a realistic picture of a situation. Other people's opinions, observations, and informed guesses can also be useful (so can your own), but be aware that these can be biased and inaccurate, and should always be checked against your facts. For reliable and valid information, you need to search out many sources. Often a person's opinion is biased, so it is not necessarily the truth. One friend may say you have no chance, so don't bother trying out for the team; another friend is sure you're a cinch to make the team. Neither of these are necessarily true—and furthermore, they're opinions or guesses that cannot be proved right or wrong unless you actually try out for the team. It's not wrong to gather opinions, but remember that they are not facts. Another friend may say you should absolutely try out—that you might have the exact skill the team needs. This is an opinion that's accompanied by a fact: that it is possible you have what the team needs.

Consider All the Possibilities, Looking at the Facts from Different Angles

What you think may not be the only way to look at a situation. There are often many explanations for things that happen. Force yourself to look at and consider them all. Life, like a badly written multiple-choice test, is often ambiguous: we search for that one right answer when there may three or four good answers. Learning to consider all of the possibilities means you recognize that ambiguous situations are not black or white. For example, say you did not make the team. Maybe the team quota was full, or there are too many players who already play your position, or an upperclassman had first dibs on the spot. Or say your friends didn't call. Perhaps they were busy doing chores, or hanging out with their girlfriends, or had family obligations.

Try looking at a situation from different perspectives. Look at it through the eyes of your friends, parents, coaches, teachers, or siblings. Consider this situation at a different point in time. What might you think about it later today, or tomorrow, or next week, next month, or next year? What would you say if a friend came to you and asked your advice on the situation?

Consider Your Past Experiences

Think back to all the difficult situations and stressors you have faced and conquered. Your past experiences can prepare you to effectively deal with the here and now. You can think back on how you handled past situations and use that information to face a current situation. This perspective can help you come up with a larger, more complete picture of the situation you're in, and can help you come up with a plan of action rather than reacting impulsively.

Be Careful Not to Jump to Conclusions or Make Broad Generalizations

The first thing that pops into your head is not always an accurate conclusion. And when a person assumes the most negative or worst of everything, it's easy to jump to the wrong conclusion. Instead of blindly accepting the first idea you have about a situation, slow down and think it through. When you don't make the team, don't assume you didn't have the talent. When your friends don't call, don't decide they don't think you're cool. Make conclusions based on the *facts* of the situation. Try to stay objective so that you don't incorrectly judge the situation with a negative bias. Be careful not to make it personal when it isn't.

Be careful also not to draw broad, sweeping generalizations based on one fact or one result. Just because you bombed one test does not mean you won't do well on the next one. Just because you weren't included this time does not mean you aren't wanted or you won't be included next time.

Understand Your Doubt Distortions

Often, when we start examining our reactions to difficult situations, we begin to notice patterns. We realize we have habits of thinking that bog us down over and over. These habits or patterns are doubt distortions: problematic, prejudicial ways of seeing situations. If you can learn to identify your own doubt distortions, you will be more and more able to shut them down before they keep you from reaching your goals.

Doubt distortions are mistakes in thinking. Thinking mistakes can contribute to your seeing situations incorrectly. Doubt distortions are unconscious, and they systematically warp how you see yourself, your relationships, and the world around you. Because it is impossible to attend to everything going on around you and within you all the time, you probably have unknowingly developed a shorthand way to walk through the world. We all do this. It's efficient, but it's prone to being inaccurate. And when your doubt is activated in any given situation, one or more of these doubt distortions may automatically turn on. The distortion actually filters out the positive and neutral information so that all you have left is negative, self-critical, or anxiety-producing information.

Doubt distortions come in a number of flavors. Check out the descriptions below and see which types you tend to use. These doubt distortions are also central to the teen stories in chapters 4 through 7. You may even find it helpful to bookmark this page so you can refer back to it later.

Extreme Thinking

When you engage in *extreme thinking,* you see yourself in terms of all or nothing. Things are black or white with no shades of gray, and it becomes impossible to accurately see the big picture. Extreme thinking is usually fueled by extreme standards. For example, Jake was playing goalie for a prestigious travel soccer team, and he gave up the winning goal. Based on that, Jake thought he played a lousy game. He lost sight of all the tough saves he made and couldn't form a realistic picture of how well he actually played.

Seeing the whole picture rather than the extreme view allows you to take the credit you deserve and share responsibility when it is warranted. Seeing only the end points gives doubt—and a negatively warped perspective on the whole—an opportunity to take over (*I gave up the winning goal, so I'm a bad player; I flubbed a line and that ruined my performance*).

Depending Only on Your Emotions

When you are *depending only on your emotions* to the point of either ignoring the facts of the situation or assuming the facts when none yet exist, you have a doubt distortion. Imagine having spent many hours studying for a test and after you take it you feel like you bombed; you think about dropping the class before the results are in. Imagine getting the results back three days later and seeing you aced it. Your reaction was based entirely on your emotions, which rushed in before there were any facts to depend on. Your emotions are also in charge when you think the person you would like to hang out with is not interested in you—even though the person includes you in plans, appears to have a good time in your presence, and keeps talking about concerts you could see together.

When you look beyond your feelings to the facts, you gain an unbiased, accurate view that frees you from unnecessary distress or from taking inappropriate action. Allowing your feelings to rule lets a doubt distortion creep in.

Nasty Name-Calling

Nasty name-calling is when you label yourself in a negative way—for example, labeling yourself stupid for not doing well on one test. Or, for another example, Alissa had been looking forward to helping out at the soup kitchen. When the day arrived, she forgot all about it, and she overslept and missed the opportunity. She called herself a loser, was ready to quit community service, and feared seeing the teacher who organized the event.

When you stop calling yourself these nasty names, you can stop beating yourself up. One mistake does not define your character. Labeling yourself negatively because you slipped up only provides fuel for doubt to grow.

Catastrophizing

When you are *catastrophizing*, you take a small, possibly insignificant situation and make it bigger and much worse than it really is. You imagine the worst-case scenario as being the only possible outcome. For example, say you don't do well on a test. You begin to believe you will fail the rest of your tests—even the whole marking period. For another example, one night many of Josh's friends were planning to go to a big party, and no one called or texted to fill him in. Josh thought no one wanted him to come to the party, and this led him to imagine sitting home alone on weekends for the rest of the school year.

Not catastrophizing allows you to keep each situation in the present and keep your thoughts event-specific. Instead of imagining untold upset and what-ifs to come, keep the situation in perspective. For Josh, it was a case of miscommunication: everyone thought someone else had told him about the party. Permitting yourself to catastrophize leads you to doubt yourself.

Forecasting the Future

When your doubt distortion takes the form of *forecasting the future,* you imagine your future in the most negative or fearful way. You operate as a fortune-teller believing you can predict the future—and the picture you have of it is bleak. Then you dwell on your unconstructive prediction—you believe it—and this causes emotional damage and compromises your choices. For example, Samantha dreamed of attending the college both of her older brothers attended. After the official visiting tour, she decided that with her credentials she would never get in, and that she would never find another school she would like as much. Samantha failed to consider more positive alternative possibilities: that her extensive community service and solid grades, along with her sibling status, might boost her chances at acceptance; or that she might wind up attending a different school that would be a better fit for her.

If you give up forecasting the future, it keeps the door for future possibilities open. Believing in the most negative or dangerous outcome lets insecurity and doubt take over.

Expecting Too Much

When you're *expecting too much,* you operate on imperatives: "must," "should," and "have to" lead to unrealistic and rigid expectations. You place constant stress on yourself trying to live up to these expectations. When you or others are unable to live up to your impossibly high expectations, frustration, anger, and disappointment are likely to follow. For example, maybe you try your hardest and practice constantly to make your color guard routine flawless, while some of your teammates seem to take it less seriously and give it less effort. You think they *should* be giving it the effort you do, and because they don't, you're angry at them. Replacing your *should* with a wish or desire is a way to reduce your distress. Instead of thinking they *should,* try thinking *it would be nice* if they worked harder, or that *you would prefer* it, or *you wish* they would. This allows you to accept that you have control only of what *you* do, and that you cannot simply demand that others cooperate. Demanding they take it more seriously is not going to help, but letting them know you wish they would work harder, or that you'd like them to, may get their cooperation.

Replacing "expecting too much" with a preference keeps doubt from getting activated. Instead of beating yourself up (or feeling helplessly frustrated with others) for falling short of your unrealistic expectations, you can take the pressure off and do what you can.

Zooming In on the Negative

When your doubt distortion takes the form of *zooming in on the negative,* you fail to see the big picture; you focus exclusively on the negatives. Your biased view leads you to draw negatively exaggerated conclusions. For example, Jack and his friends had been talking about camping out, so Jack took the initiative and planned a trip. When he was telling his friends the details, he noticed one friend rolling his eyes. Another seemed distracted by his phone. So Jack assumed no one was on board and the trip was off. By zooming in on the negative, Jack missed the positive cues, failing to see that one friend was making a list of everything he wanted to bring while another was inviting more people to come along.

Not zooming in on the negative keeps you from drawing the wrong conclusions. Incorrect assumptions give doubt an opportunity to grow.

Use Everything You've Learned to Understand the Situation

Looking at your interpretations of situations, and learning to judge what is inaccurate and what is either factual or more likely to be valid, is the start of removing doubt and building confidence. Using all of the data you can gather prepares you to correctly apply any or all of the following questions to your thinking:

1. Looking at the evidence, are your thoughts based on facts and accurate, or are they inaccurate give-up thoughts with no evidence to support them?

2. Are there other possible explanations?

3. What is the worst that could happen, and what are the odds that it will happen?

4. Would you be able to cope if the worst thing did happen?

5. What is the best possible outcome?

6. What is the most likely outcome, and how different is it from your worst fears?

7. What would you say to a friend who had doubts about this situation? What might a friend say to you?

8. Overall, what is the most reasonable way to see this situation?

Examining the truthfulness of your thoughts—especially if they are give-up thoughts—enables you to see an accurate, alternative interpretation of any specific situation. The evidence you have gathered—your facts—is the basis of your go-to thoughts. Your go-to thoughts are helpful and accurate ways of looking at any situation. Seeing situations realistically minimizes doubt, uncertainty, and unnecessary risk.

Once you have assessed whether you are reacting to a difficult situation with realistic concern or doubt, and have identified your give-up thoughts and your doubt distortions, you are in a better position to accurately assess the situation.

Recall the distinctions between realistic concern and doubt we discussed earlier in the chapter, and the clues that your thinking about a situation may be off track and based on doubt:

◆ Your thoughts are particularly negative or are riddled with fear-ful concerns.

◆ You have strong unpleasant feelings disproportionate to the situation, such as anger, fear, sadness, guilt, or shame.

◆ Your body is experiencing disagreeable symptoms, such as shaking, trembling, feeling hot, sweating, clamminess, shallow breathing, or extreme or excess pain.

If your thoughts are accurate interpretations of the situation, this means that your reaction arises from realistic concern. The steps you can take to respond include gaining whatever information, skill, or experience you need to succeed; taking corrective action if necessary; and getting help from others if it's reasonable.

Realistic concern is understandable, and it typically occurs when you are facing new situations and lack the skill, practice, or experience to deal with them easily. Realistic concern is legitimate when you are just learning a skill and haven't mastered it yet, when you lack the skill, or when you just haven't had the experience to know what to do. When you lack the necessary knowledge, realistic concern makes sense. Realistic concern also applies to genuinely difficult situations by which you may be personally and negatively affected.

Realistic concern might arise when you are:

- driving the car for the first time or navigating somewhere new

- going on your first date or to your first dance, semiformal, or prom

- taking your first standardized test

- doing an extreme sport for the first time

- starting a new job or academic course

- going to your first job or school interview

- asking for an accommodation from a boss, teacher, or other authority figure

- trying out for a sport, band, play, orchestra, or chorus

- facing a medical, psychological, or learning issue

- in the middle of a family crisis such as divorce, illness, or death

Accept that there are going to be plenty of first times or difficult situations you will face, but do not make your inexperience or lack of skill or knowledge mean something negative about you. Instead, recognize the merit of your realistic concern and work toward taking the appropriate course of action.

Action Options When You Don't Know What You're Doing

If You Lack:	You Can:
Skill	Seek out training, knowledge, or help. Use all the assistance available to you, such as teachers, computer programs, apps on your cell phone, parents, coaches, or courses.
Practice	Find opportunities to improve your skills. Join a club or team; ask a teacher or a coach for extra problems, exercises, or drills. Make the time to practice, and ask others to practice with you or practice alone.
Experience	Engage with the situation, and practice problem solving as you go. Keep in mind that there is rarely one right answer, but rather lots of answers each with its own set of pluses and minuses. Look at the pluses and minuses and choose the answer that makes the most sense with the information available. Know that if the answer that makes the most sense today doesn't work out, you can always change course and try another path.

If your reaction arises from doubt, don't let your misguided fears stop you from facing a situation. Instead, work to learn how to remove self-doubt so you don't put needless obstacles in your way or take unnecessary detours. Take notice of your feelings and bodily sensations but, instead of letting them rule, use your feelings and sensations as signals to access and learn to evaluate your thoughts.

Keys to Gaining an Unbiased View

Don't let your feelings and bodily sensations rule you.

Think about what you are thinking.

Stick to the facts.

Don't just react, think through all your options.

Give yourself credit for taking action no matter how small the step.

Keep in mind that the hardest part is often just getting started.

Don't get caught up in imaginary predictions and doubt distortions.

Try imagining yourself taking action without the burden of doubt.

Be willing to try.

Know that success is in the doing and not in the result.

EXERCISE: A Positive Picture of You

As you are learning, your *doubt belief* is your self-imposed nasty label. It is the "I'm (a) _____" that you call yourself (see chapter 1 for this). The key to effectively and permanently squashing it is to recognize that no one single characterization, weakness, nasty name, or struggle defines you forever forward. It is also important to recognize that the doubt belief is not true about you in every situation, 100 percent of the time—it simply can't be.

Your *confidence belief*, in contrast, is based on an accurate picture of you. It is developed from your many qualities, characteristics, and strengths. Use the following spaces to write down as many of these as you can come up with (use more paper if you run out of room). You possess many positive qualities that no mistake or shortcoming could possibly cancel out.

1. Write out your academic and intellectual strengths. For example: good at geometry, chemistry, poetry, digital imaging, organization; have a good memory, come up with creative ideas.

    _____

    _____

2. Write out your social strengths. For example: loyal, trustworthy, kind, good conversationalist, fun, good listener.

    _____

    _____

3. Write out your talents. For example: artistic, musical, athletic, good dancer, writer, or actor.

    _____

    _____

4. Write out your positive physical attributes. For example: nice smile, hair, or eyes.

    _____

    _____

5. Write out what you like about your personality. For example: funny, caring, serious, inquisitive, laid back.

    _____

    _____

6. Write some compliments you have received lately from people. For example: "You did a nice job" or "You look terrific."

    _____

    _____

7. Write down some other strengths you have. For example: hard worker, avid reader, good person, tech wiz.

    _____

    _____

Build Your Confidence Mindset

The preceding exercise makes it clear that no one is defined by any single quality or attribute. We are all multifaceted, complex, interesting individuals. Everyone has the capacity to be competent and capable. Being competent does not mean you can handle every task and every situation independently. It means you have the ability to figure it out or find the help you require to accomplish the task. Knowing you're capable means you feel pretty sure you'll be able to do a good enough job of handling whatever comes up.

Every one of us has what it takes to be desirable—to be loved and offer love. Accepting yourself as desirable means you believe you are a good and likeable person. It means you're unlikely to worry about being rejected or excluded, or unintentionally disappointing someone. You cannot please everyone all the time, and you are not going to be "it" for everyone. Knowing you're a good and likeable person means you recognize there will be other opportunities, other dates, and other invitations.

Paying attention to your abilities strengthens your self-confidence and arms you to defeat your self-doubt when it surfaces. Seeing the big picture and embracing all the qualities that define you are your greatest assets in growing your self-confidence and protecting yourself from self-doubt. And practicing paying attention to the parts of you that are good and likeable and competent can help keep you from interpreting situations inaccurately.

The confidence mindset is the positive, accurate, realistic way you see yourself in any given situation. It is the conclusion of your unbiased, fact-based, go-to thoughts. It is the self-confidence you carry inside you that helps you stand up to difficult situations and provides reassurance that you have no need to fear what waits ahead. Your confidence mindset is the fact-based, positive self-statements that provide you with courage. Learn to listen to them! Here are some examples:

◆ *Mistakes don't make me a failure but a human being with the capacity to learn.*

◆ *Rejection is not a reflection of my character or my future but of some particular person's preference.*

◆ *Asking for help means I know how to survive and is a sign of strength and not weakness.*

◆ *Putting my needs first some of the time means I can be the better person I want to be.*

◆ *Choosing to do what is in my interest makes me powerful and puts me in charge; this is true even if it is something someone in authority is telling me to do.*

◆ *I am a complex, multifaceted package of qualities, and I won't get caught up in any one shortcoming.*

The confidence mindset boils down to this: you are a capable, good, and likeable person.

The Bottom Line

You can turn away from self-doubt and toward self-confidence by learning to capture and examine your thoughts instead of simply buying into whatever you're thinking or feeling. By building the skills to differentiate between realistic concern and doubt, you will have the power to develop a more accurate view of yourself and the world around you. Realistic concern is an internal warning signal that you're in trouble, when the objective data for the situation indicate that your thinking is accurate. In contrast, doubt is thinking you're headed for a problem or catastrophe when there are no or limited valid facts to back it up. That's why it's so important to capture your thoughts and evaluate them, and then take appropriate action (we'll talk more about that in the next chapter). Follow these steps to understand your thoughts relative to a situation:

1. Start by calming yourself.

2. Ask whether you are experiencing realistic concern, or doubt.

3. Don't let emotions take over.

4. Look at the facts.

5. Understand your doubt distortions.

6. Use everything you've learned to understand the situation.

These steps serve as a guide to think and talk yourself through a specific difficult or challenging situation. They also give you excellent practice in replacing troublesome give-up thoughts with go-to thoughts. As you effectively squash the credibility of your self-doubt, you are also building up and continually strengthening self-confidence by seeing yourself in a more positive, accurate, and realistic way. You are learning to recognize that realistic concern is a good indicator that it's time to take action, but not to freak out, distort the facts, or beat yourself up. You'll also become more aware of the types of doubt distortions that increase your risk of making a mistake in your thinking. By being a thoughtful, thorough analyst of your own life and the world around you, you can grow your confidence belief by continually collecting accurate, reliable data about you—a capable, complex, good person. This will help to cement your confidence mindset forever forward.

CHAPTER 3

Do the Right Thing: Turning Sound Thinking into Confident Action

*"You don't have to be great to get started,
but you have to get started to be great."*

—Les Brown (musician)

Believing in yourself also means being equipped with effective skills to pursue your goals, trust you've made the right decision, and take appropriate action. Taking action is the best way to solidify your confidence. Only firsthand experience provides the facts necessary to walk the walk of confidence. When you're trying for the aced tennis shot, byline in the school paper, or lead in the play, sometimes you just have to go for it: building confidence works the same way. When you face the tough challenges in life and don't shy away from unpleasant situations—when you do things even when they're hard or uncomfortable—your confidence will grow.

The key is to go through a process in which you learn and grow new strategies and practice going after what you ultimately want without getting sidetracked by behaviors that don't work, or *ineffective actions*. Ineffective actions happen when one behavior becomes a habit used in every situation regardless of whether or not that strategy works. Think of it this way: If you use only the hammer in your tool box, you'll never be able to drill a hole, saw a piece of wood, or measure the length of any object. Would banging away at everything really work all of the time?

Ineffective Actions

There are numerous ways to respond in any situation. The behavior you choose can be helpful, ineffective, or even harmful. Your choices come from what you've learned or observed from important people in your life, situations you've been exposed to, media messages, and even suggestions you've tried or stumbled upon. But when you overuse a behavioral strategy, it leads to ineffective actions, which block your path to success.

There are three main kinds of ineffective actions:

1.   Avoidance

2.   Perfectionism

3.   Ineffective communication

Avoidance

Avoidance is not facing up to things. It's the opposite of taking planned action. Avoidance becomes ineffective action when it pulls you away from doing what's important. It's skipping out on school, an exam, a paper, practice, a party, a chore, or an interview. It can also be dodging your parents, friends, teachers, and coaches.

Here are some ineffective avoidance actions.

Avoiding

The avoider is the ultimate dodger. He evades everything and sidesteps problems, trying to get out of responsibilities. The avoider disappears into the bathroom when everyone else is helping clean up, doesn't contribute to the group project, doesn't participate in class, or misses big school events.

Quitting

The quitter gives up before trying or doesn't see it through to the end. The quitter is the one who misses the basket in a game of horse and walks out on the game before it's over. The quitter starts the paper but never gets it done, starts the test and walks out before completion, or writes the e-mail and never pushes "send."

Distracting

The distracter focuses attention away from the priority task and gets busy doing something unrelated. Watching television, eating, listening to music, or playing video games replaces staying on task. She can also distract herself and cause harm by using alcohol or drugs.

Disadvantages of Avoidance

Avoidance keeps you from dealing directly with what's important. You spend energy burying your head in the sand instead of facing the task, and you wind up with bigger problems, unfinished important work, and missed opportunities. You're at greater risk for punishment and penalties. Avoidance also means you don't put yourself out there, so you miss out on the critical positive accomplishments necessary for building self-confidence. Without the objective facts to grow your confidence, your subjective negative imagination can take over and feed your insecurity.

Read the next two situations and see if you use any of the ineffective action styles characteristic of avoidance:

1. Your teacher thought you were involved in a classroom incident you played no part in, and it will most likely affect your classroom participation grade. What do you do?

   ◆ *Avoid:* You don't talk to your teacher, and you start cutting class.

   ◆ *Quit:* You stop putting effort into your schoolwork and participating in class.

   ◆ *Distract:* You don't think about what happened; you focus on other things.

2. It's your party, but your best friend doesn't want you to include some kids you're very friendly with. What do you do?

   ◆ *Avoid:* You put off making the invite list.

   ◆ *Quit:* You decide to cancel your own party.

   ◆ *Distract:* You turn on the TV and don't think about it.

Replace Avoidance with Effective Action

Instead of using avoidance, an ineffective choice, it's necessary to change it up and use a more effective action. The avoidance habit is often one of the hardest ineffective action strategies to overcome. Avoidance feels protective, since it keeps us from facing difficult or unpleasant situations. But in the long run it leads to greater difficulty and unpleasantness. The ability to choose an effective action comes from thinking your options through and choosing the behavior or behaviors that work best for each situation. Instead of relying on one behavior, be flexible and review all your available options. There are often many effective action choices. Think about replacing your ineffective avoidance strategies with some of these effective action options:

- **Problem solve:** Define the problem; consider your options; weigh the pros and cons; pick a solution.

- **Prioritize:** Don't let unimportant distractions get in the way of taking care of more urgent items.

- **Stop the delay tactics:** No more excuses or distractions. Keep on the task.

- **Schedule in timed breaks:** No impulsive interruptions for snacks or drinks. Plan your break times.

- **Take action:** Make a plan and put it on your schedule. Tackle the task head on. Action can happen even if you don't feel like it or want to do it. Start doing.

- **Just try:** Give it your best effort and make an attempt.

- **Keep it simple:** Be clear about the task, and don't make it more complicated than it is.

- **Use help:** Try it on your own first, but use your resources if you need additional information or assistance.

- **Small steps:** Break the task down into smaller, manageable pieces so you aren't trying to start and finish a task all at once.

- **Each thing you do counts and deserves credit:** Consider writing it down so you appreciate how much you do.

- **Do it without knowing the result:** Don't let anxiety and fear of the unknown stop you before you even begin.

- **Stay focused and present:** Stay on task and focus 100 percent of your attention. It's not the time to check Facebook, text friends, or glance at TV.

◆ **Follow through:** Hang in there and see the task through until it's done.

Perfectionism

Perfectionism is demanding you get it exactly right: mistakes, flaws, missteps, inaccuracies, oversights, errors, and slip-ups are unacceptable. If you engage in perfectionism, it can dominate every sphere of your life and make you think you must be the perfect student, child, sibling, friend, athlete, musician, artist, and person. It cons you into thinking there's just one right thing to say, do, or be. Perfectionism leads to ineffective action. It guarantees you will never be good enough, since you'll always fall short of your impossibly high standards. The need for perfection makes you believe you have to be 100 percent in control and please everyone; it causes you to worry continually.

Here are some ineffective perfectionism actions.

Seeking Perfection

The perfectionist holds herself to an ideal standard. Everything must be exact, complete, right, or ideal. Falling short in any way is intolerable and unacceptable. The perfectionist is unhappy with anything less than 100 percent the way she wants it.

Controlling

The control freak has to be in charge of everyone and everything. He insists that everyone else's plans revolve around what works for him or what he wants. He makes sure it's right for him by choosing to drive, make the plans, host the events, and pick the restaurant.

Pleasing

The pleaser is all about pleasing others. In her zest to make others happy she often compromises her own needs. The pleaser is the one who volunteers to do everything and has a hard time saying no. The pleaser is afraid of not doing things just right for fear of rejection.

Worrying

The worrier is constantly troubled and anxious about things that have happened or might happen. He thinks about the worst that could happen and dwells on that possibility, but doesn't consider the best or most likely outcomes. He thinks, *What if things don't go well? What if my friend gets mad? What if I don't do well? What if something bad happens or I can't do it?* The worrier is overly concerned about things not going exactly right.

Disadvantages of Perfectionism

Perfectionism trips you up in many areas of your life. Perfection is an unhealthy goal that can't be realistically defined or achieved. You can't be in more than one place at a time, juggle all your responsibilities, and do your best in all areas at once. If you're part of a family or team, you can't be responsible for everyone else doing their parts exactly right. It's impossible to please everyone or always be in complete control. Worry doesn't change the outcome or help obtain that goal perfectly.

The remedy for perfectionism is to realize and accept that you're guaranteed to fall short in some way. Not because you're not good enough. We're all human, and each of us has our own unique set of strengths and weaknesses. Trying to be perfect gets in the way of feeling good about yourself, how you walk through the world, and your relationships. It also gets in the way of starting things. Your perfect standards demand you spend excessive amounts of time trying to do, say, or study enough to get something exactly right. It's impossible, and as a result you invest huge amounts of time and effort and never accomplish anything, or you end up thinking your efforts aren't good enough, and insecurity takes over.

Read the next two situations and see if you use any of the ineffective action styles characteristic of perfectionism.

1. Your teacher thought you were involved in a classroom incident you played no part in, and it will most likely affect your classroom participation grade. What do you do?

   ◆ *Seek perfection:* You put in so many extra hours, trying to convince the teacher you're the top student, that you sacrifice your well-being, your friendships, and your ability to take care of your other responsibilities.

   ◆ *Control:* You demand that no one around your seat speak to you in class, and you make sure to lead the classroom discussion and assigned group projects and never give anyone else a chance.

   ◆ *Please:* You bring the teacher coffee, treats, or small gifts to try and please the teacher.

   ◆ *Worry:* You keep thinking, *What if this ruins my GPA for the year?*

2. It's your party, but your best friend doesn't want you to include some kids you're very friendly with. What do you do?

   ◆ *Seek perfection:* You repeatedly try to come up with the perfect plan to force your friend to change her mind but no plan is ever good enough to implement.

   ◆ *Control:* You dictate who you want to invite, along with all the other details of the party, with total disregard for your friend's feelings.

◆ *Please:* You try to please everyone else and invite only who your best friend wants you to invite—and you lose sight of what you want.

◆ *Worry:* You worry that no matter what happens, everyone will be upset with you.

Replace Perfectionism with Effective Action

Perfectionism is an ineffective choice when you hold yourself up to such an excessively high standard that only 100 percent is acceptable. When you recognize that it's impossible to get it exactly right all the time, you can hold yourself up to a realistic measuring stick. Letting go of perfectionism doesn't mean you let go of realistically high standards for yourself. It doesn't mean your work will be second rate, or that you'll settle, slack off, or become lazy, or that people will see you as uncaring or selfish. Total perfectionism and worrying are never effective actions. Taking control and pleasing others is fine some of the time, but it can't be effective all the time. Evaluate the situation. Change it up so you make sure you use the action that best fits the circumstances. Consider replacing your ineffective perfectionism strategies with some of these effective action options:

◆ **Develop realistic standards:** Accept that in many situations good enough really is good enough.

◆ **Make a choice:** Use the information you have to make the most reasonable decision, and accept that there is no perfect decision.

◆ **Yield:** Take control some of the time but not all of the time.

◆ **Take a team approach:** Let others participate and share the responsibility.

◆ **Give up the need to always please:** Consider your needs and feelings as part of the equation.

◆ **Be logical:** Don't take care of others at the expense of your well-being.

◆ **Turn off your worry:** Focus on the facts, and know that worry doesn't keep you safe or change the outcome.

◆ **Stay in the present:** Think in the "for-now" and not in the "for-ever."

Ineffective Communication

Ineffective communication means you have not clearly expressed your message—you failed to let others know what they did was a problem for you, or how you felt, or what you wanted. With *assertive communication*, you say what you mean and mean what you say. Ineffective communication is the opposite because you passively wait for others to read your mind, or you say one thing and mean another, make a snide remark, demand answers, make excuses, skew the facts, or go on the attack.

Here are some ineffective communication actions.

Being Unassertive

The unassertive communicator is passive and holds back rather than speaking up directly. The unassertive person doesn't speak up, voice opinions, correct misunderstandings, express needs, or share feelings. She wanted a ticket to the concert, but didn't tell anyone she wanted to go. Her feelings are hurt but, when asked, she says everything's fine.

Manipulating

The manipulator gets others to do what he wants by twisting the facts or maneuvering things in a way that serves his best interest. The manipulator presents partial information, omits facts and details, exaggerates insignificant details, hedges bets, piles facts to support one side, or purposely leaves some people uninformed. He wants his parents to side with him and not the teacher, so he tells only his side of the story or purposely forgets to inform his parents that his teacher requested a phone call.

Defending

The defender feels attacked, so she makes excuses or attacks back. The defender stops listening and starts reacting. She is always on guard and ready to take action to be self-protective. Someone asks why she didn't do something and she replies it was their fault for not reminding her. She gets caught doing something wrong or forgets to do something, and she refuses to take responsibility.

Disadvantages of Ineffective Communication

Ineffective communication never directly gets your point across. This leads to misunderstandings and to your feeling unappreciated, undervalued, overworked, dumped on, taken advantage of, or not considered. When you are unassertive, you miss opportunities and your needs aren't met. Manipulating others can come back to haunt you when the facts come to light. When you get defensive, you miss out on the truth or overreact. When you're unassertive, or when you manipulate others or get defensive, you compromise yourself and your self-esteem suffers. Read the next two situations and see if you use any of the action styles characteristic of ineffective communication:

1. Your teacher thought you were involved in a classroom incident you played no part in, and it will most likely affect your classroom participation grade. What do you do?

   ◆ *Be unassertive:* Say nothing and hope for the best.

♦ *Manipulate:* You maneuver your friends and persuade them to talk to the others involved so they'll tell the teacher you played no role in the event.

♦ *Defend:* In denying your involvement you make so many excuses you look guilty while at the same time pointing fingers at everyone else.

2. It's your party, but your best friend doesn't want you to include some kids you're very friendly with. What do you do?

♦ *Be unassertive:* Say nothing but hope someone else invites them.

♦ *Manipulate:* Make it your mission to manipulate your best friend into changing her mind. You elicit the help of others behind her back to convince her.

♦ *Defend:* Alternate between making excuses and angrily explaining to your best friend why she is wrong not to let you invite others to your party.

Replace Ineffective Communication with Effective Action

Taking effective action requires the confidence to communicate clearly and say directly what you mean, think, feel, or want. When you know what you want it's easier to express yourself effectively. Instead of yielding to pressure, take the stand that's right for you. Don't let others persuade you to do things that may put you at risk, compromise your needs, or hurt others. Standing up for yourself shows you matter. All of us occasionally get stuck in the rut of using one or two action strategies out of habit. The key is to move away from what's easy and replace it with what works. Try replacing your ineffective communication actions with some of these effective communication options:

- **State the facts:** If someone's done or said something that bothers you or puts you in a compromising situation, be prepared to tell them how what they said or did affected you.

- **Speak up:** Ask for what you want, or let others know what action you plan to take. Be clear and specific.

- **Listen to others:** Acknowledging what others think, feel, or want makes them more willing to compromise.

- **Compromise:** Find a solution that works best for you and takes into account the needs of those you care about. Be willing to be flexible.

- **Be assertive:** Say what you mean and mean what you say.

- **Present the full picture:** Be accurate and straightforward.

- **Give the appropriate weight to information:** Don't exaggerate to make a point.

- **Try to see both sides:** The truth is usually somewhere in between.

- **Take responsibility:** Instead of making excuses, acknowledge your role.

- **Be objective:** Consider the facts before you react.

- **Don't blow up:** Keep your cool so you can effectively deliver your message.

The Bottom Line

Knowing you are equipped with many skills to take effective action gives you the confidence to actually take the action. Ineffective action takes place when you use one or a few behaviors repeatedly in almost every situation regardless of whether or not they'll work. Ineffective action falls into the three main areas of avoidance (avoiding, quitting, distracting), perfectionism (seeking perfection, controlling, pleasing, worrying), and ineffective communication (being unassertive, manipulating, defending).

The way to break these bad habits is to not go with your typical ineffective action but to evaluate the specific situation, knowing there are numerous ways to handle and respond to any situation you're facing. Through practicing and strengthening the many different effective action options in this chapter, you can grow your confidence, knowing you are equipped with the tools to handle whatever situation you face.

Chapters 4 through 7 explain how thoughts and behaviors are directly linked to self-doubt. As you read through the teen stories, you'll see how any situation can potentially play havoc on your psyche. In each of these stories, notice how doubt-distorted thinking leads to misunderstanding, upset, and ineffective actions. Then you'll see the analytical, fact-based approach in action, working to remove doubt-distorted bias, improve mood, and help the teens in the stories take appropriate, effective action. Equipped with the most accurate view of the situation, you'll see how teens find their way to the confidence path. This corrected understanding of the situation enables each teen to think and act in the most effective way. As a result of working each step through from doubt to confidence, a new confidence mindset is gained. Seeing the most realistic, accurate, and positive view is the confidence mindset you need to strengthen your self-confidence and build unshakable self-esteem.

CHAPTER 4

Teen Stories:
Social Life, Friendship, and Romance

Friendships and romantic relationships give us lots of chances to doubt ourselves. Even the most self-confident person can feel uncertain going after new relationships, and just about everyone feels miserable when they've been rejected or are going through a breakup. Facing difficult or unpleasant social situations is unavoidable. Everyone is going to feel nervous some of the time. But you can minimize difficulties, unpleasant emotions, and bad choices by learning to recognize your doubt and replacing it with confidence. The following stories show some common social situations. As you read them, you'll learn how to recognize self-doubt and reframe it so you can find your way to solid self-confidence.

Friendships can be a painful strain when you examine them through the lens of self-doubt. With doubt comes self-criticism—we see ourselves as falling short, and we perceive rejection. We let our insecurities monopolize how we see ourselves and our social relationships. But friendships don't have to be a source of self-doubt and stress. When you know you're a good person and can thus approach relationships with self-confidence, you won't see criticism that isn't there.

Proms, dances, and parties—not to mention pursuing romantic relationships—can be uncomfortable and provoke anxiety when you focus only on your imperfections. Doubt leads you to magnify and focus on the most negative aspects of yourself or a situation. When you persuade yourself to see the positives, you get the whole picture and the courage to go after what you want.

⬥ Morgan's Story: I Care Too Much What Other People Think

I endlessly try on clothes in my closet, searching for the perfect look. Just when I think I've found it, I decide it's not right. I think: This isn't right. I don't look good. If I don't look good, people won't like me.

—Morgan

MORGAN'S DOUBT PATH

What makes Morgan so critical of her looks and of every move she makes? The doubt distortion of *expecting too much* generates this insecurity. Another distortion, *extreme thinking,* leads her to exaggerate the importance of her appearance. Morgan also worries—an ineffective behavior based on *perfectionism* that makes her late for everything because she can't make up her mind and frets about what other people think.

Here are some perspectives that could help Morgan get off the path of self-doubt: Look at the big picture instead of zeroing in on the extreme view. Who you are is much more than what you choose to wear. All kinds of internal and external things define you. You're way more than your clothes. Consider all the possibilities: standing straight or slouched; well groomed or sloppy; smiling or frowning; making eye contact or looking down. Add your height, weight, complexion, hair color, and eye color, and you can see the factors that impact how you look and how others experience you are limitless. Sure, what we present on the outside counts, but what's inside counts even more. Consider your personality, humor, intelligence, skills, kindness, sensitivity, compassion, empathy, opinions, interests, and talents. Don't exaggerate the importance of any single item; think of yourself as a package deal.

When Morgan replaces her give-up thoughts with go-to thoughts, here's what she comes up with:

Morgan's Give-Up Thought	Morgan's Go-To Thought
This isn't right.	There is no perfect outfit or shirt. My friends don't all buy the same shirt. There are lots of good choices.
I don't look good.	The shirt or outfit I wear is not the only factor in looking good. If I accept that I am an attractive person, then what I wear has a very small part. Besides, what people think looks good is individual—otherwise we'd all end up buying exactly the same outfit.
If I don't look good, people won't like me.	What I wear is not the deciding factor in whether or not people like me.

CONFIDENCE PATH

Turn off your *extreme thinking* and needless *worry* so you can have the self-confidence to wear any item of clothing in your closet. Replace your ineffective behavior of demanding *perfection* with the knowledge that you have style and a good sense of what is appropriate to wear.

CONFIDENCE MINDSET

Let go of worrying about what you wear or what anyone might think. Focus on the positive, realistic big picture that defines you and your strengths.

⫸ *Ryan's Story: It's Uncomfortable to Initiate the Plan*

I have nothing to do tonight. I want to text some friends and see if they want to hang out or know what's going on. I think: They'll say they're busy and have other plans. They may not want to hang out with me. My friends may not want to do what I want. If I organize something and it's not fun, they'll think I'm a geek.

—*Ryan*

RYAN'S DOUBT PATH

Insecurity is what generates all of Ryan's negative thinking and stops him from texting his friends or finding out about any plans for the night. The doubt distortion of *forecasting the future* makes him imagine the worst. When Ryan labels himself a "geek," his *nasty name-calling* feeds his insecurity. By not texting his friends, Ryan reinforces his doubt, and he ends up being stuck in for the night without plans.

Here are some perspectives that could help Ryan get off the path of self-doubt: Instead of forecasting the future negatively, look at the facts to see if they support a more likely outcome. Don't forget you have a lot in common with your friends and the rest of your group. You're all looking for something to do. Some of them could be waiting for your text. Consider past experiences. Think of all the times you made a suggestion and someone said yes. There's no harm in asking. If they say yes, you made it happen! If they say no, you're no worse off than you were to begin with. You can't lose. Regardless of the outcome, believing your friends will form a negative opinion of you based on one situation is the doubt distortion of *catastrophizing*.

When Ryan replaces his give-up thoughts with go-to thoughts, here's what he comes up with:

Ryan's Give-Up Thought	Ryan's Go-To Thought
They'll say they're busy and have other plans.	I won't know that unless I text. If they do have plans, there's no reason to assume they won't include me.
They may not want to hang out with me.	We all hang out and it's cool. I can just text and see what they're up to. They'll probably want to meet up.
My friends may not want to do what I want.	Who cares? I can do what they're doing.
If I organize something and it's not fun, they'll think I'm a geek.	Everybody in the group makes suggestions at different times. Sometimes they work out great and other times they don't. When they don't, I don't think my friends are geeks.

CONFIDENCE PATH

Have the self-confidence to send the text and see what your friends are up to. Perhaps they'll want to meet up or ask you to join them in whatever they're doing. You like your friends to text you to see what's up, why wouldn't they like it if you did the same?

CONFIDENCE MINDSET

Making the call or sending the text is actually easier than worrying about it. It's worth it to put yourself out there with your friends.

⫸ Carly's Story: My Friend Is Mad at Me

For the last few days my friend hasn't been returning my phone calls or texts. She's standing in front of her locker smiling and laughing with our mutual friends, and I want to talk to her. I think: She probably won't want to talk to me. Maybe she doesn't want to hang out with me anymore. She must be mad at me. What if our friendship is done?

—Carly

CARLY'S DOUBT PATH

Carly's doubt distortion of *forecasting the future* sabotages her friendships. By not asking her friend what's up, Carly's feelings of rejection grow. She convinces herself her friend doesn't want to hang out. Worse, her doubt distortion of *catastrophizing* takes over so that one negative piece of information keeps growing into a never-ending pile of distorted negative thoughts.

Here are some perspectives that could help Carly get off the path of self-doubt: Try to be more careful not to *jump to conclusions* before you have the facts. Your mind can manipulate you into believing all sorts of untrue things. Accepting these unfounded conclusions can make you suffer needlessly and *avoid* taking effective action. Instead, *collect the facts*. Talk to your friend. Remember, there might be no problem, and even if there is, once you understand it you may be able to fix it.

When Carly replaces her give-up thoughts with go-to thoughts, here's what she comes up with:

Carly's Give-Up Thought	Carly's Go-To Thought
She probably won't want to talk to me.	I won't know until I try to speak with her in person. If I try, she'll know I care.
Maybe she doesn't want to hang out with me anymore.	I have no facts to support that and no reason to believe that's true. It's important to find out what's up.

She must be mad at me.	Maybe she is mad at me. She's moody. There's no reason to believe we can't work it out.
What if our friendship is done?	There's no point in jumping to conclusions. We've been friends a long time. Without any facts, it doesn't make sense to think the worst.

CONFIDENCE PATH

Have the self-confidence to walk over to your friend and talk to her. You won't know what's up until you're face to face. Avoiding her makes you feel worse and may even make the situation worse.

CONFIDENCE MINDSET

Face your friend. By avoiding and not dealing with it directly or by getting angry and defensive, you won't get the results you want.

⯬ *Alex's Story: Do I Really Want to Have a Party?*

I was planning a party last weekend and started to feel insecure about the details. If it goes well, I'll skyrocket in popularity! I'm excited about having everybody over, but worried it might not go well. I think: I can't decide who to invite. People are going to get upset if they're not on the invite list. If I forget someone, I won't be on their invite list next time. Maybe the party will tank.

—Alex

ALEX'S DOUBT PATH

Here, Alex's doubt distortion of *worry* is getting in his way. Alex's worries about being in charge are making him stew over what might go wrong, and this is keeping him from acting. Instead of taking the initiative, Alex debates with himself: *Do I really want to have the party?* The more he thinks about it, the more uncomfortable he becomes and the farther he gets from being the leader he wants to be. A situation that has the potential to be satisfying and fun turns into a pile of what-ifs.

Here are some perspectives that could help Alex get off the path of self-doubt: Be *careful not to jump to conclusions*. Instead of seeing the party as a test you may fail, see it as a chance to chalk up one more experience to your list of accomplishments. Remind yourself you're not alone. Use your friends to help decide who to invite. Keep it in perspective and know that your friends will be happy you were willing to be the host.

When Alex replaces his give-up thoughts with go-to thoughts, here's what he comes up with:

Alex's Give-Up Thought	Alex's Go-To Thought
I can't decide who to invite.	There's no perfect guest list, and I don't have to decide alone. All it takes is a few people to make it a party.
People are going to get upset if they're not on the invite list.	I can't invite everyone. People understand that.
If I forget someone, I won't be on their invite list next time.	Most people don't keep track. Just because I didn't invite them doesn't mean they won't invite me. Maybe they don't even care they weren't invited.
Maybe the party will tank.	Parties are rarely a bomb. All parties have one thing in common: they're better than sitting at home with nothing to do.

CONFIDENCE PATH

Change it up. Stop using the ineffective actions of trying to *control* and *please* or outright *avoid*. Have the confidence to be a leader and initiate fun. You can't invite or please everyone, so concentrate on what you *want* to do. Instead of focusing on what could go wrong or worrying about the future, be in the moment and have fun.

CONFIDENCE MINDSET

Do what you want to do, and don't let worries about what you imagine get in the way of taking action.

⦿ Ashley's Story: Why Would Anyone Want to Be With Me?

I look in the mirror and scan my body from head to toe and all I see are my imperfections. I think: People will notice my face is breaking out. Nothing looks good on me. I never know what to talk about. There's no point in going to the party. No one is ever going to want to date me.

—Ashley

ASHLEY'S DOUBT PATH

Fear of rejection keeps Ashley from going after what she wants, including happiness, because the fear falsely persuades her to avoid any opportunity where there is a possibility of rejection. The doubt distortion of *forecasting the future* fuels Ashley's worst fears and makes her believe the worst is the most likely outcome. The thought distortion of *zooming in on the negatives* gets the best of her, and she convinces herself no one will be attracted to her and so there is no sense in going to the party.

Here are some perspectives that could help Ashley get off the path of self-doubt: Stop focusing on your flaws, start *considering all the possibilities*, and take all the good stuff into account. Think of all the things that define who you are. What makes you attractive to others is different for each person you meet. Stop *avoiding*. Head to the party and put yourself out there. Putting yourself out there is the only way you'll find the people who are attracted to your qualities.

When Ashley replaces her give-up thoughts with go-to thoughts, here's what she comes up with:

Ashley's Give-Up Thought	Ashley's Go-To Thought
People will notice my face is breaking out.	No one is inspecting my face but me. Look around, everybody has acne.
Nothing looks good on me.	My clothes are fine. It's me that feels like I don't look good. Let me look in the mirror again and find some things I do like.
I never know what to talk about.	My friends talk about what we share in common. I will surely be able to add things, or I can let other people talk and be a good listener.
There's no point in going to the party.	It makes sense to go and check it out. My friends are going and I can hang out with them.
No one is ever going to want to date me.	I won't know until I put myself out there. My friends like me, so I have proof that I have qualities people find attractive.

CONFIDENCE PATH

Seeing yourself as a whole picture keeps you from magnifying your negatives. Putting yourself out there gives you the chance to find out that other people actually want to be with you.

CONFIDENCE MINDSET

Put yourself out there. Focus on your positives, and don't get caught up worrying about what you think other people might think. You don't have to fear rejection if you don't make it mean something personal.

◀▶ *Brett's Story: I Want to Ask Her Out*

She's standing in front of her locker with her two best friends. I'm totally into her and I'd love to ask her to hang out, but the last thing I want to do is embarrass myself. I think: She probably wouldn't want to hang out with me. She probably likes someone else. She's way out of my league.

—Brett

BRETT'S DOUBT PATH

The doubt distortions of *forecasting the future* and *extreme thinking* keep Brett from approaching this girl. Insecurity stops him dead in his tracks and leaves him feeling bad about himself. Brett convinces himself not only that she wouldn't want to hang out, but that no other girl would want to either.

Here are some perspectives that could help Brett get off the path of self-doubt: Relationships always come with risk. There are never any guarantees that someone you like will feel the same way about you. Instead of choosing the ineffective action of *quitting*, recognize that the short-term possibility of rejection is worth the gamble because it allows you the chance of succeeding. Life is an endless series of chances, so don't put so much weight on any one situation.

When Brett replaces his give-up thoughts with go-to thoughts, here's what he comes up with:

Brett's Give-Up Thought	Brett's Go-To Thought
She probably wouldn't want to hang out with me.	I won't know until I ask. Maybe she will say yes. Even if she says no, I have nothing to lose.
She probably likes someone else.	That's possible, but I don't know, so it's worth a shot.
She's way out of my league.	We're all in the same league. It's just a matter of whether or not we connect.

CONFIDENCE PATH

You can ask her out without being afraid of her answer. Who knows—you might actually get to hang out with her.

CONFIDENCE MINDSET

Putting yourself out there is the best way to get a chance with anyone.

◗ *Meredith's Story: I'm Afraid to Break Up*

I've been dating my boyfriend for the past five months, and I'm ready to move on. I really want to break up, but my insecurity keeps me stuck. I think: What if I'm making a mistake? Maybe I'll never find another boyfriend. Maybe people will get mad at me. I'll hurt his feelings. It'll be really uncomfortable when I run into him.

—Meredith

MEREDITH'S DOUBT PATH

The doubt distortion of *catastrophizing* convinces Meredith that her love life will be a never-ending failure. By *forecasting the future*, Meredith's bias takes over and she imagines the worst. Instead of focusing on what is right for her, she stays in the relationship even though she wants out.

Here are some perspectives that could help Meredith get off the path of self-doubt: Walking away from what's safe to what's unknown takes courage. Courage in this situation comes from knowing you're a good, decent person and that it's reasonable to end a relationship that isn't working. See this as one unique situation and not a pattern. All through life, if you can walk away from what's safe but unsatisfying, you're more likely to find happiness. You've proven you have the capacity to be in a relationship, so there's no reason to believe other people aren't out there for you in the future. Facing your *worry* is the only way to prove to yourself that your fears are unfounded reflections of doubt.

When Meredith replaces her give-up thoughts with go-to thoughts, here's what she comes up with:

Meredith's Give-Up Thought	Meredith's Go-To Thought
What if I'm making a mistake?	I'm not happy in this relationship. The fact is I'm ready to end this relationship and move on.
Maybe I'll never find another boyfriend.	There are plenty of guys around, and it's pretty likely someone is out there for me.
Maybe people will get mad at me.	My friends care about me and won't judge me over this. His friends might get mad at me, but they'll get over it.
I'll hurt his feelings.	I will hurt him more by pretending. Although he might feel bad now, he'll get over it.
It'll be really uncomfortable when I run into him.	It might be really uncomfortable at first, but it will get easier. We're both nice people; we can work it out.

CONFIDENCE PATH

Stop telling yourself what you should do and take assertive action. You can break off the relationship without being afraid of the consequences. Who knows? He may want to break up too.

CONFIDENCE MINDSET

If you don't want to get stuck where you don't want to be, have the courage to do difficult things.

◆ *Josh's Story: I Don't Want to Be Her Boyfriend Anymore*

My phone vibrates and I see a text from my girlfriend. I don't really want to answer her. We're so done, but my insecurity keeps me from telling her how I feel. I think: I'll hurt her feelings. She's a good person and I don't want to look like the bad guy. People think she's really hot; maybe there's something wrong with me.

—Josh

JOSH'S DOUBT PATH

Josh believes he should stay in the relationship even though he doesn't want to. This doubt distortion of *expecting too much* fuels his insecurity. In this case Josh answers his girlfriend immediately out of obligation; he also talks himself out of breaking up with her. Instead of paying attention to how he really feels, he gets tangled up in *pleasing,* and his own needs get lost. Thinking something is wrong with him simply because his wants are different from those of others is the doubt distortion of *nasty name-calling.*

Here are some perspectives that could help Josh get off the path of self-doubt: There are few perfectly right answers in relationships, so there are no *shoulds* in making relationship decisions. Nowhere is it inscribed in stone that you have to do anything, let alone stay in a relationship you don't want to be in. Don't let the *expecting too much* error or the *demanding should* win. We all try our best not to hurt others. *Defending* your own feelings or occasionally disappointing someone doesn't mean you're a bad person. Don't let the fear of letting someone down keep you from taking the action that takes care of you or that simply makes the most sense. When you're *unassertive*, you fail to let others know how you feel, and this deprives them of the truth and the opportunity to respond appropriately. This compromises your own needs.

When Josh replaces his give-up thoughts with go-to thoughts, here's what he comes up with:

Josh's Give-Up Thought	Josh's Go-To Thought
I'll hurt her feelings.	I wish I could avoid hurting her, but I need to do what's right.
She's a good person and I don't want to look like the bad guy.	Breaking up doesn't make me a bad person. It just means we didn't work as a couple.
People think she's really hot; maybe there's something wrong with me.	There's nothing wrong with me. It's the relationship that's not working. It happens.

CONFIDENCE PATH

You need to do what's right for you. By asserting yourself in the nicest way possible, you let someone know how you feel and what you want.

CONFIDENCE MINDSET

Don't be afraid to take care of yourself and state your needs. Do what's right for you.

⬥ *Drew's Story: I Can't Get Over the Breakup*

I thought we were so good and had such a strong bond, but after two years she told me she needed her own space. I can't believe we're done. I keep replaying the relationship in my head, wondering what I did wrong and if there's something wrong with me. I think: I'll never have that bond with anyone again. She knows me better than anyone else. This can't really be over. I keep thinking about her and can't get over it.

—Drew

DREW'S DOUBT PATH

Drew won't accept that the relationship is over, and he talks himself into thinking there's still a chance. He *avoids* making plans with friends so he can be available in case she calls. Drew tries to *manipulate* her friends to find out where she's going so he can be there to see her. He checks his cell phone 24/7 for her texts or calls; he clicks constantly on her Facebook page to see if she has changed her relationship status or if she's getting posts from other guys.

Here are some perspectives that could help Drew get off the path of self-doubt: Loss is painful. Don't be afraid to grieve. Grieving allows you to say goodbye and acknowledge that you'll genuinely miss what you've lost. Give yourself permission to grieve. Trying to avoid the grief only delays the ache. This is real loss and it's appropriate to be sad. The key is to accept that this was not your only chance at love. See this as one unique situation and not a pattern. Getting beyond grief requires purposeful action and a mind open to new possibilities. If you start putting your energy into doing what's important and what you enjoy, it will help you move on.

When Drew replaces his give-up thoughts with go-to thoughts, here's what he comes up with:

Drew's Give-Up Thought	Drew's Go-To Thought
I'll never have that bond with anyone again.	Just because it feels that way doesn't make it true.
She knows me better than anyone else.	She knows me better than anyone else right now, but that doesn't mean that someone else can't get to know me that way. If I don't put myself out there, I won't find out.
This can't really be over.	She said she needs space. There's no point in telling myself it's not over if it is. Denying the truth is only going to prolong the pain.
I keep thinking about her and can't get over it.	I can put this behind me if I focus on other things and accept that the relationship is over. Doing something fun will help.

CONFIDENCE PATH

Stop putting your life on hold waiting for her. When you stay home to make yourself available to her, when you don't do the things you enjoy, you sink your mood even further. Change your ineffective action from *avoiding* and manipulating to the effective action of speaking up. Pick up the phone. Make plans with your friends or simply make a plan to do something you want to do.

CONFIDENCE MINDSET

Know that grief is temporary. The sooner you deal with it, the sooner it will be in the past.

The Bottom Line

The key to success across all social and romantic relationships is self-confidence. Self-confidence comes from knowing you're a composite of great qualities, skills, talents, and roles. When you accept that you're a desirable package and a capable person, you won't be threatened by rejection, fear of others' judgments or opinions, peer pressure, or disappointment. Get in touch with what you genuinely want, believe in the whole person you are, and make your choices accordingly. This approach means you are being true to yourself.

CHAPTER 5

Teen Stories:
School, Sports, the Arts, and on the Job

School, sports, artistic pursuits, and jobs are all places where self-doubt can develop, grow, and get in your way. All of us have the potential to feel insecure when we perform in front of others. Facing challenges is unavoidable in the classroom, on the athletic field or stage, or in the workplace. Your experience of doubt, fear, and distress can be minimized and even avoided if you let confidence be in the driver's seat. Check out the stories below and think of how what you learn can be applied to your own life.

◆ Kelly's Story: School Is Hard

I study endlessly and put way more hours into my work than anyone else does, and yet I still struggle in class and don't get good grades. I think: I'm not as smart as anyone else in the class. It's much harder for me than others. I'm so dumb.

—Kelly

KELLY'S DOUBT PATH

When Kelly struggles, she makes that struggle a reflection of her competence or smarts. She lets it define her character, and the doubt distortion of *nasty name-calling* is activated. In this case Kelly calls herself dumb. Filled with doubt, she sits in class and wonders how she's ever going to learn the material. Ineffective action strategies of *worry, avoidance,* and wanting to *quit* dominate. Kelly spends way too much time thinking the work is impossible rather than getting the help she needs.

Here are some perspectives that could help Kelly get off the path of self-doubt: Sometimes things come easily, but other times tasks can seem overwhelming and too difficult. Acknowledge that you're facing difficulty and accept that it's hard, but don't let it be a mark on your character. Choose a more effective action strategy of problem solving and act appropriately to get the help you need. Be careful not to *jump to conclusions.* Just because your schoolwork is challenging does not mean you can't learn the material. Use the resources that you have: teacher, school tutoring, parents, and peers. Getting the help you need reflects on your resourcefulness and is a sign of strength and an excellent life skill.

When Kelly replaces her give-up thoughts with go-to thoughts, here's what she comes up with:

Kelly's Give-Up Thought	Kelly's Go-To Thought
I'm not as smart as anyone else in the class.	Just because I'm having a hard time doesn't mean I'm not smart. There are times I get the material and others don't.
It's much harder for me than it is for others.	This is a hard class and lots of people around me are struggling. Some people are doing really well, but they're the ones putting in endless amounts of hours.
I'm so dumb.	That's just not true. It also doesn't help to call myself dumb.

CONFIDENCE PATH

Who you are and what defines you are much more than your grades. You are smart and have many strengths to your credit. Stop stamping nasty name-calling labels on your head just because some academic work is a struggle.

CONFIDENCE MINDSET

Becoming aware that something is difficult is normal for all of us. It does not define you and is not a reflection of who you are.

◀ *Eric's Story: I Probably Shouldn't Do This*

I struggled with some of the math problems during my first math test and doubt my abilities. I've noticed the person next to me seems to have all the answers, and I'm thinking of taking a peek. I think: I'll never pass this test on my own. These problems are just too hard for me. I'll be in big trouble if I get caught, but I'm desperate.

—Eric

ERIC'S DOUBT PATH

Eric is tempted to cheat because he doesn't have confidence in himself. The fear of not being able to master difficult material comes from his underlying insecurity. When doubt is activated, it makes him think tasks are impossible. He's overwhelmed by wanting to take the ineffective actions of *avoiding* or *quitting*, or wanting to do anything rather than face the situation (in this case, cheating on the test). Instead of trying to do the problems, Eric listens to his doubt distortion of *forecasting the future* and concludes he can't do them.

Here are some perspectives that could help Eric get off the path of self-doubt: Once you turn off your *extreme thinking*, you can squash your inclination to cheat and finish the exam on your own. Instead of forecasting the future, don't assume you can't do the problems until you try. Instead of assuming defeat, try imagining the best thing that could happen. Beware of *catastrophizing*, take pride in doing your own work, and recognize that if the exam does not go well it is only one test.

When Eric replaces his give-up thoughts with go-to thoughts, here's what he comes up with:

Eric's Give-Up Thought	Eric's Go-To Thought
I'll never pass this test on my own.	Even though I'm afraid I don't know how to do these problems, it doesn't mean I can't figure it out—or try, anyway. Whatever the grade, at least it will be my own work.
These problems are just too hard for me.	It's only the first test. If I'm really stumped, I can get help to do better for next time. Meanwhile, I won't assume I can't figure it out until I try.
I'll be in big trouble if I get caught, but I'm desperate.	Desperation over this one test is no reason to do something that could ruin my future.

CONFIDENCE PATH

Take pride in the fact that, whatever the outcome of the exam, the work was yours and yours alone. Don't get caught up in making a decision that will undermine your self-confidence by leading you to look down on yourself.

CONFIDENCE MINDSET

Pride comes from doing your own work.

◆ Max's Story: I'll Get to It

School is so stressful. I keep thinking about all the work I have to do and putting it off. It's down to the wire, and now it seems like a Herculean task. It's too much for me to handle. I think: I'll just push it back and get to it later. I can't do this now. This is an unrealistic amount of work.

—Max

MAX'S DOUBT PATH

Instead of starting his homework, Max hangs out with his friends, watches television, plays video games, shoots hoops—anything except his waiting assignments. This procrastination shows the ineffective action of *distraction*. Putting things off creates trouble or makes things worse, actually causing the distress Max was trying to avoid. Max's belief that he can't do it and it's too much for him is the doubt distortion of *extreme thinking*, which convinces him to procrastinate without any regard for the price.

Here are some perspectives that could help Max get off the path of self-doubt: It feels like the work is insurmountable because you haven't begun. Facing a task requires you to believe doing it is in your best interest and that you have the wherewithal to tackle it. Leaving your schoolwork to the last minute is reason for realistic concern. You may in fact have more to do than you will be able to get done in the limited time you allowed. But by changing your ineffective behavior of *avoiding* the work and just doing it, the pile diminishes. At the same time, your confidence in being able to tackle it grows.

When Max replaces his give-up thoughts with go-to thoughts, here's what he comes up with:

Max's Give-Up Thought	Max's Go-To Thought
I'll just push it back and get to it later.	The only way I can stop being a procrastinator is to schedule a time to start and then do it. Avoiding just makes everything worse.
I can't do this now.	It makes sense to do my work if I want to achieve my goals. Telling myself I can't is just me conning myself. Doing my work just requires taking action.
This is an unrealistic amount of work.	It may feel like too much work, but by starting on it I'll find out it's manageable. If I wait until the last minute it really will be too much to do, but if I start now I will most likely be able to get it all done.

CONFIDENCE PATH

Remind yourself of all the times you've faced work that you didn't want to do or that seemed like too much and you've been able to handle it. Tackling work head-on is an effective strategy for getting it done, and it's a chance for your confidence to grow.

CONFIDENCE MINDSET

Putting things off is a habit you can break when you put yourself to the task and face it.

⚜ Emily's Story: Thank You for the Invite, But I Have Too Much Work to Do

A bunch of girls from my hockey team are getting together to watch movies. I'd love to hang out with them, but I'd spend the whole time sweating over the schoolwork I still have to do. I think: I'll get behind on my schoolwork if I don't do work tonight. My parents wouldn't like it if I didn't do well. I have to be perfect or I could fail. I might ruin my college options.

—Emily

EMILY'S DOUBT PATH

The clock ticks as Emily debates whether or not to go. Instead of either studying or having fun with her friends, Emily wastes endless amounts of time deliberating. Doubt makes her think anything less than *perfection* is failure, when in fact that isn't true. *Extreme thinking* biases her viewpoint, and she ends up *expecting too much* of herself. Insecurity in her abilities convinces Emily that she cannot afford to do anything but schoolwork or failure will result. Instead of balancing work and fun, she risks compromising both and spending the night frustrated and disappointed with herself.

Here are some perspectives that could help Emily get off the path of self-doubt: Don't let the doubt distortion of *extreme thinking* compromise your opportunities. Just because you strive to do well in school doesn't mean that you have to give up everything else. Grades are important, but not to the exclusion of time for friends or extracurricular interests. Sometimes having endless amounts of time to do your work means you will work less efficiently. If you make plans with friends, it may mean you use the rest of the time more efficiently.

When Emily replaces her give-up thoughts with go-to thoughts, here's what she comes up with:

Emily's Give-Up Thought	Emily's Go-To Thought
I'll get behind on my schoolwork if I don't do it tonight.	I can study this afternoon and finish tomorrow.
My parents wouldn't like it if I didn't do well.	My parents want me to do well, but not at the cost of my happiness. They don't want me to make my schoolwork so important that I have no friends or social life.
I have to be perfect or I could fail.	Demanding that I be perfect is an impossible expectation. Failing has nothing to do with a less than perfect grade.
I might ruin my college options.	Not studying one night is not going to blow my college profile. I'm a good student; having a social life won't change that.

CONFIDENCE PATH

Succeeding in life is more than good grades. Give yourself a break and have some fun. You've done an excellent job making your schoolwork a priority; it's just as important to consider your social and emotional needs.

CONFIDENCE MINDSET

Give yourself permission to take a break from your school assignments, knowing you are a good student and one night with your friends won't be the problem you're stressing over. Balance is essential.

◀▶ *Justin's Story: Will I Get Into a Good College?*

My college applications are all in, and I haven't heard from anywhere yet. I'm getting worried; many of my friends have already received acceptances, but not me. I think: I may not get accepted anywhere that I've applied. What will I do if I don't get in? Maybe I'm not smart enough or good enough. College just may not be in the cards for me.

–Justin

JUSTIN'S DOUBT PATH

When faced with the unknown, Justin imagines the worst possible outcome, *forecasting the future*, and lets *catastrophizing* turn that picture into an even more extreme nightmare. In this case, he heard others talking about their college acceptances and *jumped to the conclusion* that he is never going to get into a college where he'd want to go or, even worse, that he won't get into college at all. Instead of remaining optimistic or talking to his college advisor, Justin panics.

Here are some perspectives that could help Justin get off the path of self-doubt: Doubt has led you to jump to conclusions before you have all the facts. *Collect the facts.* Rationally, you know you have applied to a number of schools where your profile is in the usual admissions range, and that many don't let prospective students know until the spring. A reality-based perspective is that the most likely outcome is acceptance to at least one of the schools you've applied to. If the worst case occurs, you can always problem solve, taking effective action by applying to additional schools.

When Justin replaces his give-up thoughts with go-to thoughts, here's what he comes up with:

Justin's Give-Up Thought	Justin's Go-To Thought
I may not get accepted anywhere that I've applied.	I'm jumping to a conclusion without facts. No school's rejected me. For all I know, I'll get into every one. My guidance counselor made sure I applied where I want to go and where my profile is what they're looking for. In the worst case, it won't be my first choice, but that doesn't mean I won't be happy there. Besides, I can always transfer if the school isn't a good fit for me.
What will I do if I don't get in?	It doesn't make sense to start scrambling when that may not happen. If I don't get in, I can figure out what to do then.
Maybe I'm not smart enough or good enough.	Getting into college has to do with a lot of things. Just because I stress over it doesn't mean I don't look good on paper or I'm not good enough.
College just may not be in the cards for me.	If I want to go to college, there are many things I can do and resources I can consult in order to make it happen.

CONFIDENCE PATH

Don't *forecast the future*: you don't know what will happen. The realistic picture is that college is in your future. Even if a school turns you down, it doesn't mean you don't measure up.

CONFIDENCE MINDSET

Think positive; don't assume the worst. College, like most things, is attainable if you want it and are willing to be flexible in how you pursue the goal.

◈ Jordan's Story: I'll Freak Out Speaking in Front of the Class

It's the first day of class, and the teacher just announced that one of the requirements is an oral presentation. I'm panicked and pretty freaked out. I think: I'll do a bad job. I'll embarrass myself. I'll be too nervous to do it.

—Jordan

JORDAN'S DOUBT PATH

Nervousness is an expression of fear. Jordan's fear comes from believing he is facing a dangerous situation unprepared. It is the doubt distortion of *forecasting the future* combined with *extreme thinking.* Jordan sees his oral presentation in a threatening way. He believes he's in danger of messing up and making a fool of himself.

Here are some perspectives that could help Jordan get off the path of self-doubt: *Consider past experiences.* Rather than *worry*, remind yourself of all the times you've already stood in front of the class. No matter what happens, chances are it won't be the disaster you imagine. Often, facing a dreaded situation is the best way to dispute your fear. Piling up your resources equips you to face situations regardless of their threat. *Look at it from different angles*, reducing your fears by knowing everyone else has to do it too. You'll have lots of time to prepare and practice. Your most important resource is believing you are capable.

When Jordan replaces his give-up thoughts with go-to thoughts, here's what he comes up with:

Jordan's Give-Up Thought	Jordan's Go-To Thought
I'll do a bad job.	I can prepare and know my material. To feel more comfortable, I can practice in front of my parents or friends.
I'll embarrass myself.	It hasn't happened yet, so why think it will this time? Besides, my friends and I always make fun of each other. That's what we do.
I'll be too nervous to do it.	Being nervous does not mean I can't perform. Thinking about it is worse than doing it.

CONFIDENCE PATH

Talking in front of an audience is not the threat you're making it out to be. If you know your material and are prepared, you can do this. What is the worst that can happen? You're nervous and stumble over a word. No big deal. Being confident means not making this into more than it is. It's just the required oral presentation.

CONFIDENCE MINDSET

Put the danger into perspective. Believing you're capable will reduce the threat of any situation. How nervous you are does not define the outcome.

⦙ Jesse's Story: I Didn't Play Last Year, Why Bother Trying Out Again?

After two intense weeks of tryouts, I didn't make the team last year. This year the odds are better, but why bother? I might just cross my name off the list. I think: I'll never make it. I could just work out instead. Even if I make it, I probably won't get any playing time. It's not worth it.

—Jesse

JESSE'S DOUBT PATH

When coaches and team members scrutinize Jesse's performance, doubt gets in his way. The doubt distortions of *forecasting the future* and *extreme thinking* make him assume he has no chance. When Jesse listens to his feelings and chooses a course of action before he has the facts, the doubt distortion of *depending only on his emotions* takes over. In this case, he expects rejection or little playing time so he *defends*—making excuses for not trying out. When Jesse listens only to his feelings, he misses the facts: this year he has a good chance to make the team.

Here are some perspectives that could help Jesse get off the path of self-doubt: Taking a chance is often the accomplishment in itself. Trying out for the team—whether you make it or not—shows you have what it takes to reach for your goals even if you get knocked down along the way. Trying out means you have a chance. Not trying out guarantees failure. As Wayne Gretzky said, you miss 100 percent of the shots you don't take.

When Jesse replaces his give-up thoughts with go-to thoughts, here's what he comes up with:

Jesse's Give-Up Thought	Jesse's Go-To Thought
I'll never make it.	Right now I'm discouraged and sure I won't make the team, but I won't know unless I try. The odds are better than last year with so many seniors graduating and the roster expanding.
I could just work out instead.	Okay, this is an excuse to avoid trying out. It's a good backup plan, but it's no reason to miss an opportunity.
Even if I make it, I probably won't get any playing time.	Being on the team is more than game time. I love this sport, and practicing it all week with my friends is often more fun than the games themselves. Besides, if I make the team my skills will improve, which increases the odds that I'll be the one in the game.
It's not worth it.	I want a chance on the team. That means it's worth the effort.

CONFIDENCE PATH

Don't *avoid* by letting your emotions rule. Get out there and try your best. Let yourself consider the best-case scenario: you make the team. Putting out the effort may help get you noticed.

CONFIDENCE MINDSET

Go for what you want even if there's no guarantee you'll get it.

◀▶ *Anthony's Story: I Didn't Make the Team*

I spent two grueling weeks trying out for the squad, hoping to make varsity but willing to accept a spot on JV. Today, I found out that I didn't make either team. I think: I just don't have what it takes. What's the point of playing if I'm never going anywhere with this sport? I'm never putting myself through this again. I should have made the team.

—Anthony

ANTHONY'S DOUBT PATH

Disappointments happen to all of us. Anthony's constantly criticizing himself inflates his setbacks by leading to the thought distortion of *zooming in on the negative*—he assumes it is his shortcomings that kept him off the team. Anthony's doubt leads him to the ineffective action of being *defensive*—he believes the coach unfairly passed him over. His doubt distortion of *catastrophizing* (*I am never going anywhere with this sport*) makes him throw in the towel. Then what? Anthony would be giving up an activity he loves.

Here are some perspectives that could help Anthony get off the path of self-doubt: Stop zooming in on the negative and *consider all the facts*. Consider why you did not make the team *from all the angles*. There were a ridiculous number of kids trying out for a limited number of spots. Most kids would be cut. Some have been playing year-round for years; some had personal trainers working on their skills with them. Not measuring up to the best of the best doesn't mean you don't have skill or talent. Just because you aren't playing on the team doesn't mean you have to give up the sport.

When Anthony replaces his give-up thoughts with go-to thoughts, here's what he comes up with:

Anthony's Give-Up Thought	Anthony's Go-To Thought
I just don't have what it takes.	I know I can play this game. Just because I don't look as polished as the others doesn't mean I don't have skill. Most of the kids on the squad have invested more time, training, and effort into this than I have.
What's the point of playing if I'm never going anywhere with this sport?	I enjoy this sport. Just because I didn't make the team is no reason for me to stop playing.
I'm never putting myself through this again.	I wanted to play on the team, and it's okay to admit it. I'm bummed, but I don't have decide about next year now.
I should have made the team.	It would have been great to make the team. I have the same skill level as some of those who made the cuts but more things came into play when the coach chose the squad.

CONFIDENCE PATH

Trying out for the team was an achievement in itself. Think of all the hard work and time you put into it. Sure you feel disappointment in the outcome, but it's no catastrophe. Don't let the doubt distortion of *expecting too much* place unreasonable demands on the situation. Replace the ineffective strategies of *quitting* the sport or reacting *defensively*. Keep playing. Remind yourself of the reasons you didn't make the squad, but remember that none of these is a reflection of your worth as a person.

CONFIDENCE MINDSET

Don't let rejection mean any more than it does. Rejection only means that you did not get what you wanted today. It is not a forecast of what will happen in the future.

◆ *Carrie's Story: I'm Not Good at Gym*

How the heck will I make it through another gym class? The teacher clearly has it in for me and won't take another skip excuse. He already warned me that my grade is at risk. I think: I hate gym. Why do I even have to take this class? Why show up if I'm just going to get a bad grade anyway? I'm not an athlete; I'll do something to embarrass myself.

—Carrie

CARRIE'S DOUBT PATH

Like Carrie, when we are faced with a challenge, our insecurity can get activated. In this situation, Carrie imagines the worst, and the doubt distortion of *forecasting the future* kicks in. She throws in the towel rather than trying. Doubt and fear take over. Her imagination paints a picture of her being embarrassed, with the doubt distortion of *catastrophizing* being the brush. She chooses the ineffective strategy of *manipulation*—she pretends to be sick and heads to the nurse.

Here are some perspectives that could help Carrie get off the path of self-doubt: Stop *forecasting the future* and face the challenge. It's likely to be easier than you imagine. Getting a decent grade in gym has more to do with participation and enthusiasm than skill. Replace your worry about embarrassing yourself with the knowledge that your fears are imaginary. Instead of avoiding gym, consider telling your teacher about your fears.

When Carrie replaces her give-up thoughts with go-to thoughts, here's what she comes up with:

Carrie's Give-Up Thought	Carrie's Go-To Thought
I hate gym.	Gym is a means to an end. I don't have to like it. I just need to participate, show some interest, and tough it out.
Why do I even have to take this class?	Gym is mandatory. I'll survive, just like every other year.
Why show up if I'm just going to get a bad grade anyway.	Showing up gives me a chance for a decent grade. Telling my teacher the truth about my gym fears might actually pay off.
I'm not an athlete; I'll do something to embarrass myself.	Most people who love gym aren't looking at anyone else. The only one paying attention to me is me.

CONFIDENCE PATH

Instead of seeking out the nurse, head into class believing you'll do fine. Gym is much more about participation and attitude than skill. Before you assume something will be impossible, face it. Who knows? You may find that there are some gym activities you like.

CONFIDENCE MINDSET

You can do things even if they're not your strengths and you don't like them. Be willing to try before you assume you'll fail.

◀▶ Chad's Story: I Just Have to Go for It

I stare down at the jump in the terrain park as I ride the chair lift and fantasize about the perfect 540 Tail Grab I'll land. The jump calls to me even though the landing looks sketchy. Most guys stay clear, but I have to prove I can do it or they'll think I'm a wimp. I think: I don't care if it's beyond my skill: I'm going to try it. I've got to land this trick before I leave. This might be my last chance. It's all or nothing. This is how I roll.

—Chad

CHAD'S DOUBT PATH

Sometimes doubt-based behaviors can look a lot like confidence. But remember that the confidence mindset is based on a positive assessment of your abilities that is also realistic. In this case, Chad's insecurity tells him that extremes prove he's the man—it's not confidence talking at all: it's doubt. Instead of listening to the voice of reason—which tells him he doesn't yet have anywhere close to the skill he needs to land the trick—he convinces himself he needs to do it, and do it now. Chad's thinking gets skewed when he listens to the doubt distortion of *depending only on his emotions*. He impulsively heads to the jump and goes for it. His *extreme thinking* makes him believe anything less than the toughest trick won't cut it, and *expecting too much* made trying the trick feel like a must.

Here are some perspectives that could help Chad get off the path of self-doubt: Going all out doesn't mean you have to push things so far you put yourself in danger. The doubt distortion of *extreme thinking* makes you put your ego ahead of common sense, and you go for the trick. Sure, it would feel awesome if you made it, but you'll have a realistic shot at it only if you build your skills more. The cost of using an ineffective behavior—needing to *defend* your image—could be really high. You could injure yourself badly enough to ruin the rest of the boarding season and any chance of starting on your spring varsity sport. The key is to learn when you are pushing it too far.

When Chad replaces his give-up thoughts with go-to thoughts, here's what he comes up with:

Chad's Give-Up Thought	Chad's Go-To Thought
I don't care if it's beyond my skill: I'm going to try it.	I have to accept major ramifications if I don't make it. One adrenaline rush is not worth the price I'll pay for injury. Think it through and consider the price.
I've got to land this trick before I leave.	It's been such a great day, why mess it up? No one else is being that crazy. I don't have to do this trick today.
This might be my last chance.	I've been riding for years and plan to keep boarding for many more. There'll be plenty of chances for plenty of jumps and tricks. Forget about it being now or never and enjoy the day.
It's all or nothing.	I think it's either full throttle or no throttle, but that isn't true. Riding my board is a rush regardless.
This is how I roll.	Just because I tell myself this is how I roll doesn't mean I can't make a different choice. Doing things well and pushing boundaries doesn't mean I have to push beyond my limits.

CONFIDENCE PATH

Instead of impulsively yielding to your need to prove yourself to your friends, think it through and be realistic about the potential consequences. Focus on having an awesome day on the slopes and in the action-packed season ahead. Don't let one extreme act mess it up.

CONFIDENCE MINDSET

Go full throttle, but know when you're pushing yourself over the edge into danger. Don't lose sight of long-term consequences when faced with high-risk situations.

◀▶ *Sydney's Story: It's Too Much Commitment*

I've been singing in the chorus forever. I've spent years taking lessons, practicing, and performing. I'm heading into junior year and ready to quit. I don't think I can handle it all anymore. I think: It's taking away all my free periods so I can't get my work done. It's too much. I won't be able to handle it all. I won't have any time to have fun.

—*Sydney*

SYDNEY'S DOUBT PATH

Worry is an ineffective behavior. Sydney focuses on the worst possible outcome, feels overwhelmed, and starts second-guessing herself. Her fear of choosing a wrong course of action means she chooses inaction. Worry leads her to obsess about her decisions rather than thinking them through objectively.

Here are some perspectives that could help Sydney get off the path of self-doubt: Instead of worrying you don't have the time to do it all, look at what you're doing well. So far you've successfully juggled schoolwork, chorus, and friends. Decide what you genuinely want to do. *Consider past experiences.* There's no need for worry based on your track record.

When Sydney replaces her give-up thoughts with go-to thoughts, here's what she comes up with:

Sydney's Give-Up Thought	Sydney's Go-To Thought
It's taking away all my free periods so I can't get my work done.	It's true it uses some free periods, but not all. Not every class has piles of assignments. I'll find the time I need to get work done.
It's too much.	Chorus may feel like a lot of effort, but I've always been able to get my work done. If it becomes too much I can always miss a rehearsal.
I won't be able to handle it all.	I've always been able to juggle it all. Even when I thought I couldn't, I did. Rather than worrying about the future, I can look at my past experience. I know I'll be fine.
I won't have any time to have fun.	I'd like more time to hang out during the week, but I still have the weekends. Plus I get to see my chorus friends during practices and performances.

CONFIDENCE PATH

Have the self-confidence to know that you can get your work done, enjoy the chorus, and hang out with your friends. Focus on what you want to do instead of *worrying* about the problem that hasn't happened. If your schedule does get out of hand, trust that you will have the resources to do something about it then.

CONFIDENCE MINDSET

Self-confidence comes from knowing you can handle a busy schedule.

◆ *Jason's Story: Why Bother? I'll Never Be the First Chair Anyway*

I'm in the middle of practice, sitting in my typical fifth chair in the second row of the orchestra. Even the younger kid is a chair higher. I'm discouraged. Why do I bother trying? I think: Why bother practicing each piece so much when it never pays off? I'm never going to move up. I'm never going play as well as everyone else. The conductor doesn't like me.

—*Jason*

JASON'S DOUBT PATH

When Jason *zooms in on the negative* of a situation, he's unable to stay in the now and fully participate. He could relax and enjoy playing each piece of music, but instead he focuses on his inadequacies. When he's distracted by self-criticism, Jason tends to lose his focus, and he has to struggle to find his place in the score.

Here are some perspectives that could help Jason get off the path of self-doubt: *Look at it from a different angle.* Playing in the orchestra is an accomplishment. It symbolizes that you have skill and talent regardless of which chair you are. Instead of accepting defeat, change your behavior. If moving to a higher chair is important, consider practicing more or getting more lessons. Think of how much work you did to be where you are and give yourself the credit you've earned.

When Jason replaces his give-up thoughts with go-to thoughts, here's what he comes up with:

Jason's Give-Up Thought	Jason's Go-To Thought
Why bother practicing each piece so much when it never pays off?	Hearing my instrument sound good is worth the practice. When the orchestra's in synch, I'm proud. Also, if I don't practice, I could move down to a lower chair.
I'm never going to move up.	I can work harder, but even if I never move up, it still looks and feels good to play in the orchestra.
I'm never going to play as well as everyone else.	How much I enjoy playing my instrument has nothing to do with how I compare to others.
The conductor doesn't like me.	I can't assume that my position in the orchestra means he doesn't like me. Chair position is based on lots of factors.

CONFIDENCE PATH

Staying in the now means giving your instrument your full attention. Your focus may improve your playing and help you move up. Recognize that sitting in any chair is an accomplishment. It reflects dedication, perseverance, and effort—all character traits to be proud of.

CONFIDENCE MINDSET

Play for your own enjoyment and don't get caught up in your position. Recognize that playing in an orchestra is an accomplishment.

◀▮▶ *Will's Story: I'll Never Get the Part*

I'm trying out for the fall musical in school. A ton of kids have shown up, but there aren't many major parts. It's hard to audition with everyone else and not make comparisons. Compared to others, I think I fall short.

I think: I'll never get the part I want. I should just leave now. There's no point in trying out. I'm not good enough.

—*Will*

WILL'S DOUBT PATH

When facing the audition, the doubt distortions of *zooming in on his negatives* and *forecasting the future* (and imagining rejection) both make Will nervous. He thinks each person in front of him has more talent and that they'll get the decent parts. The urge to leave sweeps through Will, pulling him toward the ineffective behavior of *quitting* and running.

Here are some perspectives that could help Will get off the path of self-doubt: Don't let your fear get the best of you. When you are *depending only on your emotions*, doubt stops you from seeing how talented you really are. Choose to face the audition and think of it as an opportunity to shine. Focus on the joy of doing what you love regardless of the outcome. Believe you have what it takes to play the part. You'll audition better and have more fun.

When Will replaces his give-up thoughts with go-to thoughts, here's what he comes up with:

Will's Give-Up Thought	Will's Go-To Thought
I'll never get the part I want.	I've gotten plenty of parts in the past, so there's no reason to think I won't get one today.
I should just leave now.	It doesn't make sense to leave in defeat before I even try. I have just as much of a chance to get a part as anyone else.
There's no point in trying out.	I really want a part. I love the show, and I have no reason to believe I won't be in it. If I don't audition, it guarantees I won't get a part.
I'm not good enough.	I'm good at acting and singing. I'll give it my best and enjoy my turn up on stage.

CONFIDENCE PATH

Self-confidence comes from believing in yourself and having the skills to back up that belief. *Collect the facts:* you have talent; you've been in shows before; this director praised your work in his class; you've taken lessons to hone your craft. Don't let your insecurity get in the way. Get on stage and show off your talent.

CONFIDENCE MINDSET

Recognize your skills and believe in them. If you miss out on a part, it doesn't take away from all the praise you've received or your past accomplishments on stage.

◀▮ *Chris's Story: What If I Forget My Lines?*

For years I've devoted my free time to school plays, community theater, and chorus recitals. This year's winter production is big, and tickets are completely sold out. Despite my experience, my insecurities feed my anxiety about performing. I think: What if I stink? What if I forget my lines? What will people think of me if I mess up? What will I do if I do mess up?

—Chris

CHRIS'S DOUBT PATH

For Chris, performing in front of others is tougher because he fears the worst. His anxiety escalates when he *forecasts the future* and imagines messing up his lines. His nervousness increases when the doubt distortion of *catastrophizing* makes the consequences of a mistake more serious than they are. His insecurity makes it tougher to remember his lines. Instead of looking forward to opening night, Chris dreads it.

Here are some perspectives that could help Chris get off the path of self-doubt: Don't listen to your *worry;* instead, *collect the facts. Consider past experiences.* Think of the countless performances you've been in. Remember that they reflect your talent. So you weren't perfect or you occasionally messed up your lines. Don't forget how many you got right. A recovery from a mistake can often be better than the original. Count the times someone else flubbed a line and threw you off. Much of the time things go off without a hitch, but when they don't, odds are that only your cast mates and the director will recognize the screwups.

When Chris replaces his give-up thoughts with go-to thoughts, here's what he comes up with:

Chris's Give-Up Thought	Chris's Go-To Thought
What if I stink?	Odds are I am not going to stink. Think of all the productions I've been a part of and all the times I did well.
What if I forget my lines?	I've been rehearsing for months. I know these lines backward and forward. There's hardly a chance I'll forget them. It's more likely someone else will forget his lines and I'll have to help him recover. Either way, no one in the audience will have a clue.
What will people think of me if I mess up?	People who matter have opinions of me that go far beyond how I do in any given performance. My friends and family are supportive no matter how I do. Besides, odds are I'll do great.
What will I do if I mess up?	I'll do what any actor would: I'll do my best to recover and go on as if it never happened. If I don't make a big deal about it, no one else will either. I'm stressed about a problem that hasn't happened and probably won't. Bottom line: mistakes won't kill me; I'll have no choice but to keep going; and I'll recover just fine.

CONFIDENCE PATH

To face the stage free of fear and anxiety, recognize that you are imagining troubles unlikely to occur. Even if they do, consequences will be minimal. Remind yourself of all the successful productions you've been part of—and of all the small mishaps that become inside jokes among the cast.

CONFIDENCE MINDSET

Don't imagine trouble that has neither happened nor is even likely to happen. Focus on the fun of what you are doing, not mistakes you might make.

❖ *Ross's Story: What Am I Going to Say?*

I need an after-school job for spending money. I filled out the applications but keep putting off handing them in. I'm stressed and insecure about the whole process. I think: I don't know what to say. I don't know who to talk to. I might say the wrong thing. This might be the wrong time to walk in.

—Ross

ROSS'S DOUBT PATH

It's understandable that Ross is uneasy facing the new experience of applying for a job. Lack of experience makes any situation seem threatening. Stressed and anxious, Ross fears this situation so he leaves the applications on his desk and uses the ineffective action of *distraction*, wasting time on his computer instead of taking steps toward applying for jobs. His insecurity makes him think he won't come across well to employers, and, *forecasting the future*, he fears he will say the wrong thing and show up at the wrong time.

Here are some perspectives that could help Ross get off the path of self-doubt: Don't let walking in to apply for a potential job or asking about work opportunities threaten you. Instead of being *unassertive*, take charge, knowing that it's no big deal to talk to adults about hiring. After the first few conversations you will be a pro. Be prepared for a variety of responses. Some employers might ask you to come back; some might turn you down. Whether you get hired or not is not a reflection on whether you're a good person.

When Ross replaces his give-up thoughts with go-to thoughts, here's what he comes up with:

Ross's Give-Up Thought	Ross's Go-To Thought
I don't know what to say.	I know what to say: "I'm looking for work."
I don't know who to talk to.	I can ask anyone about a job; someone will point me in the right direction.
I might say the wrong thing.	I know how to talk to adults. What's the worst that could happen? Even if I don't get the job, it's great practice for the next interview.
This might be the wrong time to walk in.	I won't know until I head over there. If it looks too busy, I can always go back later.

CONFIDENCE PATH

Putting yourself out there on the market doesn't have to be stressful. Accept rejection as par for the course of a job search and nothing personal. You're likely to have some rejection before you land something, but eventually you will get hired. Use your self-confidence to go after the job you want, knowing you're capable of doing good work there.

CONFIDENCE MINDSET

Don't think you can't make it happen before you even try. Think about it as a "for now" job and not a forever career.

✦ Kimberly's Story: It's Not Fair That I Have to Work

Between school, sports, and my social life, how can I be expected to work, too? I'm working two weeknights and all weekend, and my boss keeps calling at the last minute to get me to come in earlier or on a day I'm not scheduled. I think: I can't handle it all. It's not fair; I won't ever have a social life. I won't be able to get it all done.

—Kimberly

KIMBERLY'S DOUBT PATH

Predicting failure when there's no evidence to suggest concern is the doubt distortion of *forecasting the future*. Kimberly is *catastrophizing* when she believes she will never have a social life. *Extreme thinking* makes her sure she can't handle it all. She cancels plans with friends rather than pushing the time back or rescheduling, because her insecurity makes her think she can't handle things. Kimberly tries to *please* her boss and is *unassertive* when she does not speak out about how much she can work.

Here are some perspectives that could help Kimberly get off the path of self-doubt: *Collect the facts* and look at the big picture. You're actually doing well at school, sports, your social life, and your after-school job. Doubt stops you from seeing that you're getting it all done. Doubt stops you from seeing how capable and competent you are. Life is busy and you can handle it, but if work demands more than you can deliver, be prepared to use the effective behavior of *assertive communication* and set limits.

When Kimberly replaces her give-up thoughts with go-to thoughts, here's what she comes up with:

Kimberly's Give-Up Thought	Kimberly Go-To Thought
I can't handle it all.	My schedule works. It's jammed, but I have time to take care of my responsibilities and hang out with my friends.
It's not fair; I won't ever have a social life.	It feels unfair, true, and I wish I didn't have to work, but if I want money to spend with my friends and buy the things I want, working is a necessity.
I won't be able to get it all done.	I've been able to get everything done, and that won't change. Worry distracts and doesn't help. I feel best when I stay focused and fully attentive in each role. If I really can't do it, I'll let my boss know that I can't pick up that extra shift.

CONFIDENCE PATH

Realistically, you wouldn't be involved in all of these things if you weren't able to handle it. *Look at it from different angles*: you have Mom's approval, the boss's respect, your coach's positive feedback, and friends who want to be with you no matter how available you are. All this is proof you can handle it. Assertively telling your boss you can't cover extra hours demonstrates that you can manage difficult situations.

CONFIDENCE MINDSET

Pride comes from making your own money and knowing you can tackle a busy schedule effectively. Assertive communication also adds a certain measure of control and is a very useful skill to have in life.

✦ Nat's Story: My Boss Is Unreasonable

After months of trying, I finally found a job as a restaurant server. I'm supposed to be at work at 4:30, but my varsity game was rescheduled for today. I know it will make me really late. I dread calling my boss, and I put off calling out of fear of his reaction. I think: I don't know what to say. I don't want to face him. I'm afraid to tell him the truth because he may fire me. He's going to think I'm just lazy. There's nothing I can do.

—Nat

NAT'S DOUBT PATH

Unassertiveness is the inability to communicate the truth to another person directly. By not using assertive communication, Nat allows his boss to draw inaccurate conclusions about his intentions and behavior. In this case Nat's unassertiveness keeps him from making an important call to let his employer know when he can get there and why he's going to be late. His ineffective *avoidant* action puts his job at risk.

Here are some perspectives that could help Nat get off the path of self-doubt: Accept that your boss is not out to get you and you will be less intimidated and feel more able to contact him assertively. When you tell the truth and provide details, it prevents your employer from *jumping to conclusions*. Let him know right away. Sure, he might be frustrated or disappointed, but instead of wondering where you are, he'll know he needs a replacement. You're likely to keep your job. You're not powerless. Making that phone call puts you in control of your situation.

When Nat replaces his give-up thoughts with go-to thoughts, here's what he comes up with:

Nat's Give-Up Thought	Nat's Go-To Thought
I don't know what to say.	I can tell him the truth about my game schedule and how late I'm realistically going to be.
I don't want to face him.	I can face this call even if it makes me uncomfortable and I dread it. My stress is probably worse than the actual phone call.
I'm afraid to tell him the truth because he may fire me.	*Not* making this call is more likely to get me fired. Telling my employer the truth shows him I'm conscientious and considerate. It raises my chance to keep working.
He's going to think I'm just lazy.	If I don't call, he'll imagine all sorts of things that aren't true. I know my excuse is legit even if he questions my word.
There's nothing I can do.	There *is* something I can do: I can call work and tell my boss exactly when I can get there and why I'll be late.

CONFIDENCE PATH

Accepting that things come up that you have no control over does not mean you're powerless. When you recognize the problem—you'll be late for work—and assertively address it by calling your employer, you've taken control of the situation. Addressing real problems reminds you of how capable you are. Practicing assertive communication will make it an easier task in the future.

CONFIDENCE MINDSET

Being assertive means you have faced a situation and communicated it honestly and directly. Opportunities to be assertive boost your confidence and make it easier to face difficult conversations.

The Bottom Line

The key to success across all situations that have to do with performance is confidence. Knowing you're capable raises your self-confidence and equips you with piles of internal and external resources to face any situation, from easy to stressful. Your internal resources travel with you 24/7. From your intelligence, personality, know-how, common sense, artistry, and athleticism to your communication skills, past experiences, logic, mechanical aptitude, creativity, humor, and problem-solving skills, your internal resources grow every time you exercise them. At the same time, your external resources—friends, family, teachers, coaches, tutors, roommates, and other safe, appropriate acquaintances—wait in the wings to help you out. When you are armed with your internal and external resources, self-confidence reigns.

CHAPTER 6

Teen Stories:
Home Life and Family Relationships

Often, the seeds of doubt take root and grow first in family relationships. The verbal and nonverbal messages we get from our family shape and impact our self-view. At home we can be ourselves, taking off our armor for the day, and family members see us for who we are. Our parents and siblings know how to push our buttons, making us vulnerable to self-doubt. Knowing your Achilles' heel can help you stay clear of those feelings. Learn to pay attention to all the *positive* verbal and nonverbal messages your family uses to boost your self-confidence: they might be your greatest allies.

⫸ Ethan's Story: My Parents Are Demanding Too Much

My parents are both professionals and push me into academically rigorous schedules and extracurricular interests to boost my resume. My older brother sets a high bar. I feel the pressure to excel. My parents are setting me up for failure by encouraging me to do things beyond my ability. I think: I'll always fall short of their expectations. I'm the dumb one in the family. I'll be the only failure in the family. Why do they want me to take on work they know I can't handle? If I take on anything difficult, I will fail for sure.

—*Ethan*

ETHAN'S DOUBT PATH

When doubt discourages you, pressure to perform can be intimidating. But regardless of external pressure from Ethan's parents, his greatest stress comes from his internal uncertainties. Doubt convinces Ethan that he will fall short. Using the doubt distortion of *nasty name-calling*—labeling himself "dumb"—makes him feel ill equipped to face his academic work. Ethan convinces himself he can't succeed, and the doubt distortion of *forecasting the future* makes him see failure ahead. Discouraged about his abilities, Ethan chooses the ineffective behavior of *quitting* without trying.

Here are some perspectives that could help Ethan get off the path of self-doubt: *Be careful not to jump to conclusions.* Ask yourself if your parents are demanding or simply encouraging you to perform. They probably have more confidence in your abilities than you do because they see what you can do. *Collect the facts* and consider the data that show you can and do handle difficult work. It's not unreasonable to take the test and see whether you qualify for the higher-level course. If you don't qualify, no one expects you to take an advanced course you aren't equipped to handle—that would be unreasonable. Instead of *depending on your emotions* as a guide for your actions, let the facts guide you. Feeling like you can't tackle your schoolwork does not mean you can't. Instead of concerning yourself with your parents' expectations, ask yourself what you want for yourself. Make sure doubt doesn't interfere with reaching for what you want.

When Ethan replaces his give-up thoughts with go-to thoughts, here's what he comes up with:

Ethan's Give-Up Thought	Ethan's Go-To Thought
I'll always fall short of their expectations.	My parents believe in me because they've seen my work and know I can do more than I give myself credit for. They don't demand: they encourage me to do what will help me succeed. My parents have always said all that matters is that I give it my best effort; give it a shot. They will be disappointed only if I don't try.
I'm the dumb one in the family.	It's true that my older brother excels. The truth is there are things that each of us is better at. In fact there are plenty of things I'm better at than most people. If I stop calling myself nasty names and pay attention to what I do well, I'll see I have of my own talents and abilities going for me.
I'll be the only failure in the family.	Just because I might take a different path from my parents and my brother doesn't mean I can't succeed at what I choose. Instead of convincing myself ahead of time I'll fail, I can put myself out there and discover where I'll find success.
Why do they want me to take on work they know I can't handle?	I'm the one who thinks I can't handle the work. My parents believe I can do things that I think I can't. They point out all the evidence that says I can do more than I think. Maybe I can try a little of their confidence on myself.
If I take on anything difficult, I will fail for sure.	I'll never know what I can achieve unless I try.

CONFIDENCE PATH

Turn off the *extreme thinking* and know that success and failure are not all-or-nothing packages. It's possible to struggle or only partially accomplish a goal without *jumping to the conclusion* that you've failed. Success does not require perfection. Struggling with a specific task or academic work does not earn you the *nasty name-calling* label of "dumb" or "failure"; it means only that that specific task is hard for you. Instead of choosing the ineffective behavior of *quitting*, take a risk and try the difficult stuff. At worst, it doesn't work out. Your parents push you to achieve more than you aim for because they have confidence in you. They're not encouraging you so you'll fail, but rather so you'll have the courage to try.

CONFIDENCE MINDSET

Look at your parents' expectations as encouragement instead of demands. When they push, consider them your personal cheerleaders. Success is in the doing, not the outcome.

⬥ *Jonathan's Story: My Parents Don't Like My Friends*

My parents don't like the crowd I hang out with. Recently some of these kids have been getting into trouble at school and with the law. My so-called friends have started to leave me hanging out to dry while I have their backs. When my parents confront me about my friends, I'm always making excuses for their behavior and defending them. Now I'm starting to question my own judgment and doubt my friendships. I think: I must have been brainless to think these were my friends. I won't fit in with any crowd. If I accept that my parents are right, it means I can't make good decisions.

—Jonathan

JONATHAN'S DOUBT PATH

Hearing advice or feedback from his parents is tough for Jonathan because he sees that information as criticism. The doubt distortion of *extreme thinking* makes him think the worst: that he will never fit in. His insecurity is reflected in *nasty name-calling* when he labels himself "brainless." Instead of *looking at it from different angles* and seeing the truth in his parents' view, Jonathan digs in his heels. He tries to *defend* his position and his friends when *collecting the facts* would make it clear that he needs a new plan to expand his friendships.

Here are some perspectives that could help Jonathan get off the path of self-doubt: Listening to your parents doesn't mean you're not in control. Instead of ignoring this *information from another source*, use it as one piece of data to help you formulate a broader perspective. Your parents have objective data: they notice which friends show up on time, keep a commitment, make eye contact with others, and are polite and pleasant to be around. They're also aware when your friends antagonize others, destroy property even if only in fun, disregard house rules, are sloppy and inconsiderate of you and your things, or show up at inappropriate times. Your parents care about invitations that might get you into trouble. Listening to your parents' feedback is a sign of a confident outlook. It means you accept you're still the one in control but that you're making your choices wisely, basing them on facts, not on insecurity. Instead of using the ineffective behavior of defending your friends at all costs, put energy into healthy and reciprocal friendships.

When Jonathan replaces his give-up thoughts with go-to thoughts, here's what he comes up with:

Jonathan's Give-Up Thought	Jonathan's Go-To Thought
I must have been brainless to think these were my friends.	We were good friends, but they've changed their behavior. I'm not brainless, but sticking with this crowd is risky.
I won't fit in with any crowd.	I have plenty of other friends who accept me. The truth is I'm smart and fun. This kind of thinking is just an excuse to avoid putting energy into making new friends.
If I accept that my parents are right, it means I can't make good decisions.	Heeding my parents' advice is evidence that I *can* make good decisions. Everyone uses information from others all the time—even rocket scientists do.

CONFIDENCE PATH

Using your parents as a resource means you're open to *looking at it from different angles* and capable of using appropriate resources. You open your mind to the facts when you listen to their feedback. Have the self-confidence to change direction, knowing you can connect to all kinds of people, including friends who provide healthy, reciprocal relationships. Show you're a good decision maker and can take care of yourself by choosing a wise course of action.

CONFIDENCE MINDSET

Self-confidence means you can walk away from unhealthy friendships. Listening to others' advice demonstrates self-confidence.

⬧ *Mari's Story: It's Not Fair*

My older sister is a talented artist who spends lots of time in her studio preparing her portfolio for college. My twin brother is always on the soccer field and has a car at his disposal. Just because I'm not a creative genius or an athlete and lied about hanging out at the mall, my mom has me babysitting my younger brother 24/7. I'd like an after-school job, but I feel like the family slave, always being yelled at and blamed for everything. What's wrong with me that there's such a double standard? Everyone else gets respect, leniency, and freedom while I'm restricted and criticized. I think: My parents think I'm no good. I have nothing going for me. My parents hate me. They have no respect for me. It's totally unfair that I have to do all the work around here.

—Mari

MARI'S DOUBT PATH

The doubt distortions of *nasty name-calling* and *extreme thinking* are biasing Mari's view. She thinks she's no good and has nothing going for her. Since Mari is not an artist or an athlete, insecurity tells her that her parents must think she is no good. She *jumps to the conclusion* that her parents won't give her freedom to do what she wants. It's tough for Mari, because it's not her choice to be the solution to a problem; and it feels even worse because she lets her parents' demands demoralize her. Instead of asserting herself and asking for privileges, she *manipulates* the situation to gain freedom. She lies and sneaks around, often maneuvering to be somewhere different from where she said she'd be. Mari *unassertively* stomps off to her room and slams the door whenever they start asking her to do something.

Here are some perspectives that could help Mari get off the path of self-doubt: *Collect the facts* and *consider all the possibilities.* Your parents tell you they love you. It's possible that all of their restrictions are coming from their own anxiety that you'll put yourself in harm's way. They know your sister is safe in her studio and your brother on the soccer field, but because you have no structured itinerary they worry you'll get into trouble. You know you're a good kid and have enough self-respect not to make bad decisions, but you haven't communicated this to them. They need your help with your younger brother, and they'd rather pay you than a stranger. The fact that they rely on you suggests they trust and respect you more than you realize. Stop being unassertive. Getting more freedom won't happen if you continue to sneak around and lie. Freedom comes from being direct and using effective, *assertive communication* with your parents to negotiate a plan that works for them and as well as you. Have the confidence that you can talk to them and make a compelling case instead of assuming your situation is hopeless.

When Mari replaces her give-up thoughts with go-to thoughts, here's what she comes up with:

Mari's Give-Up Thought	Mari's Go-To Thought
My parents think I'm no good.	Just because I'm not like my brother or sister doesn't mean my parents think I'm no good. I gave them reason to fear I won't make good decisions, which led to restrictions on my freedom. If I start talking openly to them, they'll know me better and they'll more likely listen to my needs.
I have nothing going for me.	I have lots of friends, decent grades, and a real knack for fashion. I have things going for me—just not the same things as my siblings. In fact, if I talk to my mom about my interest in fashion it's possible she'll have ideas of how I could get into the industry. Instead of comparing myself to other people and zooming in on the negative, I can remind myself of my strengths.

My parents hate me.	My parents tell me they love me, so how can they hate me? It feels like it when they yell at me, but mostly they yell because I'm stubborn and won't talk to them. I admit they want to trust me, and I make it tough when I lie and sneak around. Maybe if I actually play by their rules I might get more of what I want. It sure seems to work for my brother and sister.
They have no respect for me.	My parents feel disrespected because I won't give them direct answers and don't always tell them the truth. Respect goes both ways. It's possible that if I show them more respect, they'll respect me more. I respect myself because I know I can make good decisions, so I need to try telling them that.
It's totally unfair that I have to do all the work around here.	I do get paid for all the work I do. I get that they'd rather pay me than someone else. If I try assertively telling them how I feel and what I want, maybe we can find a compromise.

CONFIDENCE PATH

Consider the fact that your parents show you they trust you and respect you by leaving your younger brother in your care. It's just not true that your parents are taking advantage of you. They pay you for your work. They went out of their way to give you a sixteenth birthday party. This demonstrates their respect and love. Instead of assuming your parents are against you, hate you, and won't let you do anything, have the confidence to assert yourself and let them know how you feel and what you want.

CONFIDENCE MINDSET

Being assertive by telling people how you feel and what you want is a sign of confidence. Confidence grows when you consider positive explanations for your parents' behavior.

⬢ *Becca's Story: My Sister Is the Favorite*

My older sister is the favorite. She's better than me at everything—she has better grades and she's a star in the pool. My parents always put her in charge and give her more freedom. I'm always in her shadow and never feel good enough. I think: My parents favor her over me. I can't compete, so why try? I'm inadequate. Everything is so much easier for her.

—Becca

BECCA'S DOUBT PATH

Walking in the shadow of a successful sibling is tough. Becca's doubt distortions cause her to make comparisons and question her abilities to measure up. She ignores the facts and *depends only on her emotions,* convincing herself that her parents favor her sister. The doubt distortion of *nasty name-calling* leads her to label herself as "inadequate," and by *zooming in on the negative,* she believes everything is harder for her. She *forecasts* that she will never shine in her own spotlight and will always be overshadowed by her sister. Instead of taking action toward success, Becca *worries.*

Here are some perspectives that could help Becca get off the path of self-doubt: *Consider all the possibilities* and you'll see that your parents treat each of you differently because you are different people, not because one is better. Their praise for your sister is not an insult to you. *Collect the facts,* and remind yourself of all the praise and recognition you've gotten, too. Accepting that she's two years older and has more privileges than you doesn't mean you won't gain them in the future. Stop making comparisons and focus on your own strengths. Don't call yourself nasty names like "inadequate" just because you have to work hard.

When Becca replaces her give-up thoughts with go-to thoughts, here's what she comes up with:

Becca's Give-Up Thought	Becca's Go-To Thought
My parents favor her over me.	My parents have different expectations for us. When I really think about it, I know it boils down to an age thing, not a favoritism thing.
I can't compete, so why try?	I make it a competition; the fact is it's not. My sister and I both have strengths, but we're different.
I'm inadequate.	I'm not lacking or deficient but different from my sister. Who I am is enough, even if I don't excel everywhere my sister does.
Everything is so much easier for her.	I know it seems that way right now. I need to remember the times I didn't have to work hard, and what it was like for my sister when she was my age. Also, I have to remind myself of all the times she's struggled.

CONFIDENCE PATH

Instead of *jumping to the conclusion* that you will never be able to compete with your sister, recognize that it's not a competition. *Consider another possibility:* that your sister and parents are rooting for you. See them as allies rather than adversaries. Think of how much better you'll feel when you stop comparing and start navigating your own path in life.

CONFIDENCE MINDSET

Similarities and differences make each of us unique and special. Self-confidence comes from seeing your family as your cheering section rather than your opponent.

◆ *Allison's Story: I'm Stuck in the Middle*

I sat in my room trying hard not to listen to the arguing going on around me. My sister and dad were fighting again, and I knew that for the next hour there'd be screaming, crying, and doors slamming. My pattern is to jump into the middle and try to make peace or fix it. I worry that I'm not being a good enough daughter or sister if I don't make it right. I think: I'm responsible for everyone's happiness. If someone is upset, it's my fault. I have to fix it.

—Allison

ALLISON'S DOUBT PATH

Allison can't see that it's impossible to be responsible for another person's happiness. The doubt distortion of *expecting too much* makes her think it's her job. Unable to fulfill this expectation, Allison takes the blame and tries to *control* the situation.

Here are some perspectives that could help Allison get off the path of self-doubt: Instead of continuing to jump into the middle of their argument, it's time to let them handle it on their own. Their argument doesn't mean anything about you as a person or a family member. It's unrealistic to expect that you can control others. Let them work things out without you. Instead of letting the way everyone around you feels determine how you feel about yourself, *collect the facts*. See all the data that say you're a responsible person even if you don't try to fix their situation.

When Allison replaces her give-up thoughts with go-to thoughts, here's what she comes up with:

Allison's Give-Up Thought	Allison's Go-To Thought
I'm responsible for everyone's happiness.	If I'm responsible for my own happiness and I don't hold anyone else responsible for it, then it's impossible for me to be responsible for someone else's happiness. I'm in charge of myself and others are in charge of themselves.
If someone is upset, it's my fault.	I don't have to blame myself for things that are not my doing.
I have to fix it.	It's not my issue. It's between my dad and my sister. This is their pattern, not mine. It's not my direct relationship with either one that needs to be fixed.

CONFIDENCE PATH

Stop *depending solely on your emotions* and know this argument is between the two of them with no room in the middle for you. You're responsible for your end of your own relationships, but not what's between the two of them. Accept that you don't have to fix other people's problems or be responsible for their happiness, and your self-confidence won't be unfairly compromised.

CONFIDENCE MINDSET

Have the self-confidence to know you can only control what *you* think, how *you* feel, and what *you* do.

◈ Zach's Story: I Don't Want to Mess Up My Relationship Like My Parents Did

I thought my parents would be together forever. I knew they didn't always get along and there was tension between them, but I never thought they would split up. Now they're getting divorced. It's turned my life upside down. I worry this will mess me up for future relationships. I think: I might do something wrong and end up like them. I question what I'm doing in my relationship and if I'm headed for trouble I don't even see. Maybe it's not possible for two people to make it forever. Maybe it's my fault they're getting divorced.

—Zach

ZACH'S DOUBT PATH

Doubt makes Zach fear he'll repeat his parents' mistakes. When Zach imagines trouble in his own relationship, the doubt distortion of *forecasting the future* reflects the insecurity in his judgment. Zach's ineffective action of *worrying* allows his fear to nag him. His self-blame comes from his own uncertainty and makes him think he played a role in his parents' divorce. Trapped by insecurity, Zach is likely to be afraid to take appropriate action in his own future relationships.

Here are some perspectives that could help Zach get off the path of self-doubt: Your parents' breakup is one unique situation, not a verdict on marriage. Just because your parents weren't able to make their marriage work doesn't mean you've inherited some sort of divorce gene. You may be able to learn what undermines a relationship by objectively reviewing your parents' situation. Note the problems, then use the information to guide you in your own relationships. Have confidence that you'll make better decisions with this insight. *Look at it from different angles*, and remember they had lots of problems unrelated to you. It's true that raising teenagers can put pressure on a marriage, but divorce is rarely a result of one stressor. More often, incompatibility grows over a lifetime. Stop *depending solely on your emotions* so you don't take blame for something that's not your doing.

When Zach replaces his give-up thoughts with go-to thoughts, here's what he comes up with:

Zach's Give-Up Thought	Zach's Go-To Thought
I might do something wrong and end up like them.	There's no guarantee any relationship will last, but just because my parents' didn't doesn't mean I won't be successful. I can boost my chances by choosing someone I'm truly compatible with, and who I respect and love. I can also work at being a good partner by being a trustworthy, affectionate, and fun companion.
I question what I'm doing in my relationship and if I'm headed for trouble I don't even see.	My parents' problems were visible. They fought all the time, and you could cut the tension between them with a knife. They didn't share interests and rarely did anything together. In fact, they preferred to be with us than with each other.
Maybe it's not possible for two people to make it forever.	Just because my parents didn't make it doesn't mean marriage can't work. My grandparents have been together forever, and that negates this belief. Besides, even though some couples don't make it, plenty of couples do. I want a life partner, so I can't give up before I try—that would guarantee I'll never reach that goal.
Maybe it's my fault they're getting divorced.	I was a small stressor in a marriage full of unhappiness. The truth is I probably had nothing to do with my parents' problems. They both have said their problems had nothing to do with my sister or me. They repeatedly tell us how much they love us and that they will be there regardless of their breakup.

CONFIDENCE PATH

Collect the facts and consider the more realistic view that you were not to blame for your parents' breakup and divorce. Accept the real reasons your parents' relationship was destined for failure and that you and your sibling played no role. Have the self-confidence that you know how to make a long-term relationship work, and stop *forecasting the future* and *worrying* about your abilities. Appreciate the wisdom you've gained from your parents' mistakes. Use it to bring confidence to your future relationships.

CONFIDENCE MINDSET

Just because your parents' relationship failed doesn't doom your future relationships. Don't take blame for things that aren't your doing.

◀▶ *Alicia's Story: I Don't Matter*

My parents are divorced, and now Mom's getting serious with her boyfriend. Lately it seems like he's always at our house. They try to include me, but I feel like I don't matter as much to her. I lose sleep about what will happen to my relationship with Mom in the future. I think: She doesn't care that we don't do that much stuff together alone anymore. He's more important to her than I am. I don't matter anymore.

—Alicia

ALICIA'S DOUBT PATH

When divorce fractures families, new relationships often come into play. Alicia's insecurity is letting her feelings take over. The doubt distortion of *depending only on her emotions* makes Alicia think her mom doesn't care about her and that she doesn't matter. She *jumps to the conclusion* that she's not important just because her mom is developing a new relationship. Alicia sulks about her situation and remains *unassertive*.

Here are some perspectives that could help Alicia get off the path of self-doubt: Change is not easy for most people. Remember it took you a while to get used to your parents' separation and divorce. It will also take time to increase your comfort as your mom gets more serious with her boyfriend. She's always made it clear you're her priority, so there's no reason to *jump to the conclusion* that you don't matter. Now that you're older and often out with friends, she has more time and energy to put into this relationship.

When Alicia replaces her give-up thoughts with go-to thoughts, here's what she comes up with:

Alicia's Give-Up Thought	Alicia's Go-To Thought
She doesn't care that we don't do much stuff alone together anymore.	When I look at it objectively, the truth is that I'm not home all that much. She still asks to do stuff, and in most cases, I'm the one saying I can't.
He's more important to her than I am.	I'm still important to Mom even if her boyfriend's becoming very important to her, too.
I don't matter anymore.	That's simply not true. If I really want to spend more time alone with Mom, all I have to do is ask.

CONFIDENCE PATH

Know that your mom's time and investment in her new relationship is not a reflection of any lack of feelings or value for you. Be careful to make conclusions that are relevant only to the data at hand. Mom's interest in her boyfriend just means she likes this man. If you miss time alone with Mom, let her know. Make the extra effort to make it happen. Use direct, *assertive* communication to talk to her so you can be crystal clear on where you and her boyfriend stand in her life.

CONFIDENCE MINDSET

Just because you think it or feel it doesn't mean it's true. Have the self-confidence to check out the facts. Assertively letting others know your feelings and goals reflects and nourishes your self-confidence.

❖ Lily's Story: Will I Wind Up as Crazy as Mom?

For as long as I can remember, Mom has been unable to participate in ordinary life. She often spends days on end in bed, leaving household chores undone. She leaves me on my own to fend for myself. I'd like to invite friends over or encourage my parents to attend things like school functions. Instead I go out of my way to keep my home life a secret. I carry Mom's illness inside me as a dark secret and fear people will find out. I think: I can't let anyone know how bizarre my mom is. People will think less of me if they see how crazy she is. I can't invite my parents to anything or my friends will wonder why my dad is always there without my mom. I'm afraid I'm going to be just like her one day.

—Lily

LILY'S DOUBT PATH

Insecurity activates Lily's doubt distortion of *catastrophizing*. This convinces Lily that others will judge her negatively based on her mom's illness and also that one day she'll wind up just like her mom. Her fear that others will judge her makes her *avoid* and shy away from intimacy. This interferes with her ability to have social relationships. Lily's friends sometimes get the wrong message when she doesn't invite them over. It looks as though she doesn't want to hang out when in fact she does.

Here are some perspectives that could help Lily get off the path of self-doubt: *Collect the facts* and think about what draws you to other people. Typically, your attraction to someone else is not based on what the rest of their family is like. If you were to critically examine any of your friends' parents, you might find plenty of unlikeable, impaired, or odd people. Would that keep you from liking your friends? Your friends like you for who you are, not who your mom is or isn't. Your friends base their opinions of you on all the assets you bring to the friendship. Qualities like intelligence, humor, personality, friendliness, kindness, compassion, and listening skills attract people to you. Have the self-confidence to know that regardless of who your mom is, your friends will like you. Recognize that you are not your mom. *Consider past experiences* and all the ways you're different. Know that just because she's unable to handle life doesn't mean you're destined to walk the same path.

When Lily replaces her give-up thoughts with go-to thoughts, here's what she comes up with:

Lily's Give-Up Thought	Lily's Go-To Thought
I can't let anyone know how bizarre my mom is.	I don't have to hide who my mom is, because no one cares. If I told people about her, I might find I'm not the only one in this situation. Think about all the other impaired parents out there—alcoholics, prescription drug abusers, and nonstop worriers.
People will think less of me if they see how crazy she is.	People base their opinions of me on who I am, not who my mom is. It's time to stop fearing others' judgments. If someone thinks less of me because of my mom, that's their problem and a poor reflection on them, not me.
I can't invite my parents to anything or my friends will wonder why my dad is always there without my mom.	It's possible no one will notice Mom's not there. Even if they do, so what? Tons of parents come without a partner. Think of how many are separated or divorced, or out of town, or just didn't want to attend. It's unfair to deprive my dad of participating in my life just because I'm afraid of what people will think.

I'm afraid I'm going to be just like her one day.	I am not just like her. There are tons of ways I'm different from Mom. I'm not depressed, in pain, or glued to my bed. Stop looking into the future and seeing trouble that isn't there.

CONFIDENCE PATH

Stop the ineffective actions of *avoiding* and *worrying* and take a different course of action. Invite your friends over or invite Dad to your school events. Know you're valued for who you are, not judged on the basis of your family members. Stop hiding and be open about her, and you'll likely be rewarded with support from your friends and increased self-confidence. Don't *forecast the future*. Accept that your mom's disabled, but don't believe it suggests something about you or your future, because it doesn't.

CONFIDENCE MINDSET

Self-confidence means you recognize your assets and don't fear others' judgments. Have the confidence to know that who your family is doesn't reflect on who you are.

The Bottom Line

You can successfully navigate your home life. As you grow the skill of seeing yourself in a positive, accurate, and realistic way, you'll continue to fortify your self-confidence. You deactivate doubt buttons when you understand what they are and effectively turn them off. Update your self-view to the person you are now, so that you recognize how much you have grown.

CHAPTER 7

Teen Stories:
Tough Stuff—Peer Pressure, Trouble, and Tragedy

Dealing with tough stuff is difficult for anyone, and the stress can activate self-doubt. But your self-confidence does not have to be affected by tragic life events: it's doubt that heightens the intensity through self-blame, self-criticism, second-guessing, and playing painful situations over and over in your head. When you make upsetting events mean something about yourself or see your role in a negatively biased way, tough stuff gets tougher. Allow yourself to stay objective and realistic rather than subjective and emotionally biased. Then self-confidence can carry you through the difficult times.

◈ *Suzi's Story: I Don't Feel Well*

My absences and late slips are piling up. I didn't plan this, but every morning's like jumping hurdles. Plus missing school made me fall behind in my work. Mom's tried to help by getting doctor's notes, but she's tired of making excuses for me and insists I pay the penalty for my behavior. The alarm goes off in my room each morning and I know I should get out of bed, but I feel too overwhelmed with all the makeup work and exams. I think: I'm too far behind; I can't face class. I'm not feeling well—I'd better stay home. It's too overwhelming. I'll never get the work done unless I stay home and catch up.

—Suzi

SUZI'S DOUBT PATH

Avoidance keeps Suzi from facing what she finds difficult. She chooses to avoid because her doubt distortion of *catastrophizing* convinces her not to face the school day. Doubt steals her confidence. Suzi uses the ineffective behavior of *manipulating* to convince her mom to get her a doctor's excuse, but it backfires. She stays home missing classes, can't get caught up, and feels more overwhelmed.

Here are some perspectives that could help Suzi get off the path of self-doubt: Change your ineffective strategies of avoiding and manipulating. Face school. Instead of *depending on your emotions,* which leads you to think school is too overwhelming, take an objective view. Staying home or arriving late doesn't pay off. Instead of catching up on assignments and missed tests, you fall farther behind and have to scramble even more to get it all done. *Collect the facts.* When you finally sit down to do the work, you will find that you can. Not facing it makes school seem harder than it is. Grow your self-confidence by getting to school on time and facing your classes every day.

When Suzi replaces her give-up thoughts with go-to thoughts, here's what she comes up with:

Suzi's Give-Up Thought	Suzi's Go-To Thought
I'm too far behind; I can't face class.	Even if my work's not done, it makes sense to go to class. Missing more classes only puts me farther behind. It's stressful in class without my work done, but facing up and addressing it with my teacher will prove I can face discomfort and not let it get in my way. Facing it will be easier if I focus on what the teacher says, not on the work I blew off. Being there shows the teacher I care about her class, which makes her more receptive to my needs.
I'm not feeling well—I'd better stay home.	Telling myself I don't feel well is an excuse. I'm fine. If I'm wrong and I really am sick, I can go to the nurse and head home early.
It's too overwhelming.	Every class I miss makes it seem more overwhelming. The sooner I face my work, the less overwhelming it will be.
I'll never get the work done unless I stay home and catch up.	The reality is I won't get the work done if I go to school late, since I spend the time sleeping. It's easier to go to school and find out exactly what I need to do to finish the assignments. Making a realistic study plan will make it more likely it will get done.

CONFIDENCE PATH

Recognize that *avoidance* and *manipulation* strategies sabotage your progress, get you farther behind, and increase your overwhelming feelings. Instead of avoiding and trying to manipulate your mother, face your day with self-confidence, knowing you can handle your work if you simply get in there and start tackling it. Put a plan together, set multiple alarm clocks, and use your family members as a resource to make getting out of bed and going to school more likely to happen.

CONFIDENCE MINDSET

Facing the school day is a chance to grow your self-confidence. No matter how far behind you are, if you choose not to avoid, things will get easier.

⊛ *Emma's Story: I Can't Stop Worrying*

I've been a worrier forever. I fear I won't do well, so I think I have to work harder than everyone else. Even socially I worry about making someone upset or mad at me. Facing something new is the hardest. Now I'm about to join a sorority, and my insecurity has taken over. I think: What if no one accepts me? What if they think I'm weird because I don't drink? What if this gets in the way of my schoolwork and my grades suffer? Am I doing the right thing? It's not normal to feel this way.

—Emma

EMMA'S DOUBT PATH

Facing new situations can be stressful. This is especially true for Emma, who lets her doubt distortions of *forecasting the future* and *nasty name-calling* make her believe she'll be rejected and called weird. Emma's doubt makes her think a new fun opportunity is a source of risk. The ineffective behavior of *worry* compounds her fear. Her worry keeps Emma from fully participating. It affects everything—her schoolwork, her fun, and even her sleep. Now worry makes Emma question her decision to join the sorority and to wonder if her feelings are normal.

Here are some perspectives that could help Emma get off the path of self-doubt: Replace *worry* with the facts. Think of all the decisions you've made in your lifetime to get where you are now. You're a successful college student who loves school, friends, and family. Instead of fearing rejection, focus on the positive facts. Despite not drinking, you've been invited to join a popular sorority. Take this as proof you've been making good choices. There is no reason to second-guess yourself now.

When Emma replaces her give-up thoughts with go-to thoughts, here's what she comes up with:

Emma's Give-Up Thought	Emma's Go-To Thought
What if no one accepts me?	I've already been accepted; it's too late to be rejected. These women have invited me to pledge their sorority because they want me around.
What if they think I'm weird because I don't drink?	I am not the only underage person who's elected not to drink. They knew this before they invited me to join, so why think it'll be a problem when it hasn't been yet?
What if this gets in the way of my schoolwork and my grades suffer?	I've spent my whole life worrying about my grades. It's time to recognize I've needlessly tortured myself with this worrying. My study skills won't disappear just because I joined a sorority.
Am I doing the right thing?	Joining a sorority is something I've been looking forward to for ages. I've explored my options, and this particular sorority is exactly where I want to be a member. My choice makes total sense. There are no guarantees for the future, but for now it's right for me.
It's not normal to feel this way.	Worry doesn't have to get the best of me. Worry can signal me to pay attention to possible problems, but the act of worrying is a bad habit that will torture me forever unless I learn to turn it off.

CONFIDENCE PATH

Stop second-guessing your decision to join the sorority, and have the confidence to recognize that your choice is backed by facts. Think of all the good decisions you've made in your lifetime and how successful you've been as a result. Substitute your negative forecasts with the more likely positive outcome. Replace your ineffective behavior of worrying with action and participate fully in pledging the sorority.

CONFIDENCE MINDSET

Self-confidence means you are able to be secure in your decisions. You will not need to worry if you believe in your abilities.

◀◊▶ *Chelsea's Story: I'm Afraid to Drive*

The week I turned sixteen I passed my vision and driving tests and received my learner's permit. Of course I started nagging my parents to let me drive. Then my mom's accident changed everything. I was sitting in the front seat when a gas-guzzler rear-ended us. We're okay but the car was wrecked. It's been a month since the accident, and even though Mom keeps asking me to drive, I worry about my own abilities and make excuses so I don't have to drive. I think: I'm too nervous to drive. I'm not going to be a good driver. I could get into an accident. I don't really need to drive. There is no rush; I'll drive when I feel more comfortable.

—Chelsea

CHELSEA'S DOUBT PATH

It's understandable that a car accident would shake Chelsea up and make her question her abilities. The doubt distortion of *depending on her emotions* tells Chelsea that she's too nervous to drive. The doubt distortion of *forecasting the future* makes her imagine more car accidents, and driving becomes something to *avoid*. Chelsea relies on the ineffective behavior of *defending* through excuses to avoid what she fears. Insecurity magnifies her fear and makes Chelsea question her abilities until she's convinced herself she can't handle driving.

Here are some perspectives that could help Chelsea get off the path of self-doubt: The car accident wrecked your objectivity. Before the accident, you assumed you'd be a good driver—and the few times you were behind the wheel proved it. You drove without difficulty and enjoyed the feeling of being in control of the car. You proved to yourself and your mom you're a good driver, but the accident unleashed unfounded doubt. To regain your confidence, ask yourself if this is one unique situation or a pattern. Remind yourself that driving is a skill you'll master, and the sooner you drive, the sooner you'll believe this is true. Recognize that your mom got right back behind the wheel and told you the accident made her a safer driver by making her more alert and careful. The same can be true for you.

When Chelsea replaces her give-up thoughts with go-to thoughts, here's what she comes up with:

Chelsea's Give-Up Thought	Chelsea's Go-To Thought
I'm too nervous to drive.	My apprehension is making me nervous, but if I just get behind the wheel it will pass. Besides, being nervous doesn't mean I can't drive. Being nervous actually makes me more alert and safer.
I'm not going to be a good driver.	Why should I think I won't be a good driver? I've learned all the traffic laws and plan to follow them. Plus I've already proved I can drive a car. Being a good driver just takes practice, so the sooner I get behind the wheel the sooner I'll become a good driver.

Chelsea's Give-Up Thought	Chelsea's Go-To Thought
I could get into an accident.	Just because I could have an accident doesn't mean that I will. My mom has driven for forty years and this was her first. I can take precautions to reduce my chances. I can drive the speed limit; come to a complete stop at stop signs, intersections, and traffic lights; yield to oncoming traffic; and know what's going on around me by checking my mirrors and keeping my eyes on the road.
I don't really need to drive.	I don't need to drive, but I want to drive. Driving gives me the freedom to go where I want when I want and not wait for a ride. I'll get to sleep later in the morning if I can drive myself to school. Plus it will remind me forever that I conquered something that made me uncomfortable.
There is no rush; I'll drive when I feel more comfortable.	Feeling uncomfortable is not a reason to avoid driving. The only way I'll ever feel better is to get behind the wheel. The longer I delay the harder it's going to be. Now's the time. I know I'll feel great when I master this.

CONFIDENCE PATH

Get behind the wheel so you can replace doubt about your driving skill with self-confidence. Confidence will grow with every mile you tackle. Don't let unnecessary fear lead you to ineffective *avoidance* and stop you from doing what you really want. Remind yourself: being nervous or uncomfortable is not a reason to avoid or an excuse to give in to your unfounded insecurity. All the courage and confidence you felt driving before the accident is being overshadowed by ineffective doubt. Getting behind the wheel will remove the self-doubt so you can regain your courage.

CONFIDENCE MINDSET

Self-confidence comes from putting yourself in situations that make you uncomfortable or nervous and learning you can handle them.

⚜ *Harry's Story: I Don't Want to Drive Like an Old Lady*

Sometimes I worry that other people think I'm not cool because I'm a safe driver. I've had my license for only a few months, so I take it slow out on the road. The last thing I want is to get in an accident, dent up my car, hurt anyone, or get a ticket, so I'm careful not to speed. But my friends and even my younger brother nag me to go faster. When I drove them to the movies today, they told me I drive like an old lady. I feel pressured to go faster (which seems cool to others), but I really want to drive safely. I think: I'm a wimp because I'm a safe driver. I don't want to get in an accident, but I also don't want people going around saying I drive like an old lady.

—Harry

HARRY'S DOUBT PATH

Harry is feeling peer pressure and it's causing him to choose the ineffective behavior of *pleasing*. His insecurity is giving his peers greater influence. Instead of assertively behaving in accordance with his values, Harry speeds up, even though it makes him uncomfortable. He lets concern over not being a wimp get in the way of doing what he wants, what he's comfortable with, and what he knows is right.

Here are some perspectives that could help Harry get off the path of self-doubt: Being cool is about being true to who you are and not wimping out under peer pressure. Your values and good judgments make you who you are. Listening to others' poor judgment jeopardizes your sense of identity. Sticking to your values and beliefs makes you stronger and keeps you and those you care about safe. It makes sense to be proud of conservative safe driving, not self-conscious about it. Refusing to let anyone push you into a dangerous situation reflects ultimate self-confidence.

When Harry replaces his give-up thoughts with go-to thoughts, here's what he comes up with:

Harry's Give-Up Thought	Harry's Go-To Thought
I'm a wimp because I'm a safe driver.	Yielding to dumb goading is more wimpy than choosing what I want to do and what I know is best. Besides, since I'm not a wimp, what I do in this specific situation can't make me one.
I don't want to get in an accident, but I also don't want people going around saying I drive like an old lady.	Why care what people say if I take pride in what I value? It's possible they'll make dumb remarks, but who really cares? If it gets a laugh, what's so bad about that? I can laugh with them and not let it control me.

CONFIDENCE PATH

Don't yield to peer pressure. It's important that you realize whatever they say or do won't change your character. Have the self-confidence to drive in a way that makes you comfortable and keeps you safe. Instead of pressing the pedal, keep to the speed limit and know you're the one in charge. Don't get caught up in the doubt distortion of *nasty name-calling*—safe drivers are not wimps.

CONFIDENCE MINDSET

Having confidence means you have control of what you want to do and you don't let others dictate your actions. Who you are is a reflection of how you feel about yourself, not someone else's judgments.

◆ *Butch's Story: It's Just a Joke*

Four of us are hanging out in a friend's room taking turns checking our Facebook pages. One friend's ride arrives and he takes off. Shortly after, the rest of us realize he didn't log out of his account. One laughs and starts typing away. "Check this out," he says as he posts a crude statement on our friend's wall. I want to tell him to not to click "share," but I worry about what the others will think of me. I think: They'll think I'm a baby if I don't go along. I'm no fun. I'm being a downer. I want to fit in.

—*Butch*

BUTCH'S DOUBT PATH

Butch's doubt distortion of *extreme thinking* tells him that in order to fit in, he must play along with a prank that's actually a serious mistake. The doubt distortion of *catastrophizing* makes Butch believe his friends would judge and reject him if he doesn't participate in their dicey behavior. If he's silent, he'll be choosing the ineffective behavior of *pleasing* others, and he'll compromise himself. Butch's need to fit in and his doubt distortion of *depending on his emotions* both threaten to blind him to the potential consequences of his behavior and the behavior of his friends.

Here are some perspectives that could help Butch get off the path of self-doubt: Instead of using the ineffective behavior of *unassertiveness* and staying quiet, speak up and stop this prank. When you remind yourself that you're fun and stop *calling yourself nasty names*, like "baby" or "downer," you won't get caught up in *worrying* about what these guys might think. Help them consider what's ahead for the victim and how any of you would feel if the prank had been done to you. Having fun doesn't include hurting other people. Risking your values is a dangerous trade-off in seeking acceptance. The courage to speak up and stop your friends from having fun at the expense of another person signals self-confidence.

When Butch replaces his give-up thoughts with go-to thoughts, here's what he comes up with:

Butch's Give-Up Thought	Butch's Go-To Thought
They'll think I'm a baby if I don't go along.	The truth is that I'm not a baby, and what they think can't make me what I'm not.
I'm no fun.	I am fun. I'm as fun as any of them, but I don't have to be mean or hurtful at the expense of others. I want to stop this prank, but that doesn't mean I'm not fun.
I'm being a downer.	I'm being a good friend and not a downer when I stop my friends from making a mistake and keeping our other friend from getting hurt. Being the voice of reason is not a bad thing.
I want to fit in.	Of course I want to fit in, but not at the expense of my values. If I put a stop to this, it's less likely that any of us will be the recipient of this type of prank.

CONFIDENCE PATH

Have the self-confidence to stand up for what you know is the right thing to do. Choose the effective behavior of assertively putting a stop to this prank before it happens. The peer pressure you feel actually comes from within you—it's your ineffective action of *pleasing others* that's at work. Don't let your own insecurity convince you to participate in something wrong just to fit in. In the long run, feeling good about yourself pays off more than validation from just going along with the crowd.

CONFIDENCE MINDSET

Make the right decision regardless of what others do. Recognize that the pressure you feel comes from your own insecurity, not from the peers around you. Feeling good about yourself regardless of anybody else's opinions will grow your self-confidence.

⊪ Scott's Story: I Can't Let Them Know It Bothered Me

At our friend's house with three others, I forgot to log out of my Facebook account when my ride arrived. An hour later, someone else called to ask why I'd post such a gross comment about myself on my wall. It didn't help that Mom got the same news feed as my four hundred other friends. Mom blames me for something I didn't do, but I'm even more upset that my friends played this prank on me. I think: Maybe my friends really think what they wrote about me is true. Other people are going to think what my friends wrote about me is true. People are going to think I'm a weirdo. Even my mom thinks I wrote this poison. I have to play along or my friends will think less of me.

—*Scott*

SCOTT'S DOUBT PATH

The doubt distortion of *catastrophizing* makes Scott think he has to go along with the joke and act as if it's not a problem so his friends won't think less of him. Instead of telling his mom that he didn't write what was posted on his Facebook wall and letting her know how upset he is, Scott uses the ineffective behavior of *unassertiveness* to give her the false message that he doesn't care. Not laying out the truth to his mom about his friends means she can't help him navigate the situation. Ultimately, it gives his friends permission to do this prank again—if he pretends it doesn't bother him, how can they know how serious and hurtful it was?

Here are some perspectives that could help Scott get off the path of self-doubt: When unpleasant things happen, it's reasonable to get upset. Don't be afraid to feel bad, but when you give in to the thought distortion of *catastrophizing*, you intensify your negative emotions. Even if you don't delete the post right away, it's likely most people won't see it. Letting your friends and mom know you're upset shows you care about what they did and helps your friends recognize the inappropriateness of this behavior. Consider deleting the comment, then posting an apology for your friends' rude behavior. See your desire to protect your personal integrity as a sign of self-confidence.

When Scott replaces his give-up thoughts with go-to thoughts, here's what he comes up with:

Scott's Give-Up Thought	Scott's Go-To Thought
Maybe my friends really think what they wrote about me is true.	The point is they weren't thinking; they were just making a rude joke at my expense.
Other people are going to think what my friends wrote about me is true.	Fortunately, no one takes the news feed seriously. In fact, most people won't even see it, let alone read it. Even if they do, one nasty comment doesn't discount who I am.
People are going to think I'm a weirdo.	I'm not weird. One inappropriate remark can't make me into something I'm not. My other friends will know somebody other than me wrote it—especially if I post an apology and explanation after I delete the post.
Even my mom thinks I wrote this poison.	Not letting my mom know how upset I am reinforces her false conclusion and might make her jump to conclusions in the future. Telling her the truth and showing her I care will pay off in the long run.
I have to play along or my friends will think less of me.	Playing along guarantees more of the same in the future. If I say something now, I prevent myself and others from future embarrassment. I can't get caught up in what they think when it comes to protecting myself from bullying.

CONFIDENCE PATH

Have the self-confidence to be assertive with your friends and mom. Tell your friends they let you down and betrayed your trust. When they wrote the mean, inappropriate message on your wall, it put you in an awkward and embarrassing position. When you let your friends know, you show them you believe in yourself. Letting your mom know how upset you really are also tells her that you have values and integrity and gets her back on your side. In the long run, you will gain the trust and respect of both your friends and your mom when you speak up for yourself.

CONFIDENCE MINDSET

Letting others know when they've upset you means you value yourself. Denying your feelings is yielding to self-doubt. Being honest about your feelings shows self-confidence.

Jami's Story: Being on My Own Is Overwhelming

Growing up, I never really spent any time away from home. Now I'm a freshman in college with a roommate I don't know. I barely know my way around campus, and I feel uncomfortable joining activities alone. I don't know if I can handle college. I think: I try to make friends, but it's just not working out. I don't fit in here. I'm the only freshman having a hard time. I don't know where to start. There's no way I can stay on track academically and have a social life, too. I'm not cut out for this.

—Jami

JAMI'S DOUBT PATH

New situations filled with unknowns spark emotions. Jami's emotions spiral out of control when she lets doubt talk her into believing she can't handle the situation or that she is never going to make friends. Doubt colors the way she's looking at her college experience: the doubt distortion of *extreme thinking* convinces her that she doesn't fit in, or that she will never do okay or have a social life. Jami makes her first few rough weeks a reflection of what her entire college experience will be. She *zooms in on the negative*, focusing on the lack of new friendships and ignoring anything positive. The doubt distortion of *depending* only *on her emotions* tells Jami she's not cut out for college before she's truly considered the facts.

Here are some perspectives that could help Jami get off the path of self-doubt: Many people get homesick. It's unlikely you're the only one. Instead of letting your emotions convince you college is not for you, look at these early weeks as a transition that will improve over time. Taking effective action improves your chances of making this work. Encourage your roommate to join you in activities. Sign up for all the freshman events, even if it makes you uncomfortable to go it alone. Think of all the other freshmen in your same shoes. *Consider your past experiences* and use the skills that got you through high school and into college. Stop *zooming in on the negative* and appreciate the good things—like how nice your roommate is, and the helpful resident assistant on your floor.

When Jami replaces her give-up thoughts with go-to thoughts, here's what she comes up with:

Jami's Give-Up Thought	Jami's Go-To Thought
I try to make friends, but it's just not working out.	I'll give it time. I've been here only a few weeks. If I hide in my room, I'll never make friends. My roommate is in the same boat. I could drag her out with me. Joining a club or sorority could change everything.

I don't fit in here.	I have to give it time. It's too soon to make strong conclusions. With all my interests, there's no reason to think I can't fit in. I just need to find my niche.
I'm the only freshman having a hard time.	I'm not the only homesick freshman. Getting active and involved in campus life might be the cure.
I don't know where to start.	School is filled with students who could turn into friends. I can't meet anyone staying in my room, so it's important to spend more time on campus. I can hang out in the library, at the food courts, at sporting events, or on the quad. I can even check out some student organizations, campus activities, and sports leagues.
There's no way I can stay on track academically and have a social life, too.	Face reality: I'm overwhelmed because I'm living on my own for the first time. I know I'll be fine once I adjust to college life. In fact, it's awesome that no one's telling me what to do and how to do it.
I'm not cut out for this.	I can't say that based on just a few tough weeks of transition. I won't know what will happen until I totally put myself out there and try. I wouldn't have been accepted into the college if they didn't think I was capable of succeeding here.

CONFIDENCE PATH

Just because you feel overwhelmed in a new situation doesn't mean you aren't equipped to handle it. Focus on the facts. You're the same person who successfully made it through high school with the same study and social skills very much intact. Being homesick will pass, but pushing yourself to take a more active role in your own happiness will get you there quicker.

CONFIDENCE MINDSET

Recognize that your feelings are "for now" and that you won't feel this way forever. Self-confidence comes from believing in yourself and developing your independence.

◀▮▸ *Bri: I Don't Want to Gain Weight*

I'm an excellent student, carrying a heavy load of honors courses, writing for the newspaper, and playing a varsity sport. In addition to team practice, I run four miles a day, seven days a week. I've given up foods like cookies, cake, chips, ice cream, and bread. In the past four months, I lost thirteen pounds, which puts me at the lowest end of the acceptable weight for my height. My parents nag about my excessive need to exercise, rigid eating, and ongoing weight loss. I tell them I want to keep my weight normal, have energy, and be strong; but thinking about missing even one day of running or eating even one bite of fattening food makes me anxious. I think: I have to run. Running is the only way to reduce my stress. I'll get fat if I don't run. If I don't run today, I won't be able to motivate myself to do it tomorrow. If I eat anything fattening, I'll lose all control. I can't stand how I feel when I don't run or when I eat too much.

—Bri

BRI'S DOUBT PATH

Bri is constantly questioning her abilities and thinking she's not good enough, leading her to place unrealistic *perfectionist* goals on herself. Demanding that she run every day and eat only lean foods is the doubt distortion of *expecting too much.* The doubt distortion of *depending only on her emotions* makes her think she can't tolerate the feeling of not running or eating too much, and this compounds her fears. Bri sticks to the ineffective behavior of complete *control,* demanding perfection and believing she must sacrifice to take care of herself.

Here are some perspectives that could help Bri get off the path of self-doubt: The key is to be less rigid and loosen up the demands you place on yourself. Your fear of losing control has no basis. *Collect the facts.* You've been a disciplined athlete as long as you can remember, and you've never been overweight or eaten excessively. In the past you've eaten all kinds of food moderately with no weight issue. Eating less and exercising more actually works against you. You're more tired than ever, feel weak, are losing more weight than you want to, and live in constant fear that if you break this rigid pattern you'll morph into a couch potato. The sooner you break the pattern, the healthier you'll be. Freedom comes from the ability to be flexible and recognizing that you have options. Get confident. Skip a day of exercise. Eat forbidden food. Prove to yourself you can survive. Remember, your inflexible course is hurting your body and raises the risk of injuries and fractures. Plus it compromises everything else in your life. Have the confidence that you can stay fit and lean even without unbending rules.

When Bri replaces her give-up thoughts with go-to thoughts, here's what she comes up with:

Bri's Give-Up Thought	Bri's Go-To Thought
I have to run.	The problem is that I believe I have to run, not that I actually have to. Missing one day won't ruin my fitness. In fact, a day off will actually make me stronger, since it gives my body a chance to recover and regenerate.
Running is the only way to reduce my stress.	The demand to run every day regardless of my schedule or my needs actually builds stress. There are probably lots of other ways to reduce stress I have yet to try.

Bri's Give-Up Thought	Bri's Go-To Thought
I'll get fat if I don't run.	My weight's a result of both my diet and my exercise level. Excessive running takes off too much weight, and that's a problem, too.
If I don't run today, I won't be able to motivate myself to do it tomorrow.	Why would I stop running if I miss one day? If I think back, there are times I missed and still exercised regularly. I run not only to be fit and lean, but because I enjoy it. It's likely I'll always be a runner.
If I eat anything fattening, I'll lose all control.	I used to eat everything my mom cooked and I never had weight or overeating issues. Being so strict compromises my nutritional health, makes me frail, and weakens me at practice. Restrictive eating creates more stress and more headaches.
I can't stand how I feel when I don't run or when I eat too much.	I'll be stressing over fear of this discomfort forever unless I face it now. I feel like I can't stand the discomfort, but the reality is I can. Discomfort isn't dangerous or painful. It's just a temporary unpleasant emotion that will pass.

CONFIDENCE PATH

Choose an effective behavior and be flexible. Accept your parents' invitation to join them for dinner, and make yourself skip running once in a while. Stand up to your discomfort and choose what's in the best interest of your body and mind. Believe in yourself. Know you'll continue to exercise, run, and eat healthy even if you allow a more reasonable, flexible schedule. Moderation keeps you healthier and more balanced.

CONFIDENCE MINDSET

Self-confidence means you can count on your determination to meet your goals without being rigid and inflexible. Balance and moderation are key.

⬧ Glen's Story: I Don't Have ADHD

My parents dragged me to a doctor who said I had ADHD (attention deficit-hyperactivity disorder). They want me to consider medication plus talk to my advisors and teachers about my struggles, but I don't want anyone to think I'm a psych case. I think: Everyone will think I'm some psych case. I don't need help. People will think less of me if I have this. There's something wrong with me.

—Glen

GLEN'S DOUBT PATH

Facing any diagnosis can be intimidating. Glen's fear builds when he makes too much of the diagnosis. In this case, *forecasting the future*, Glen imagines his friends and teachers will think less of him. He looks at his problem with the doubt distortion of *nasty name-calling* by calling himself a "psych case." Doubt tells Glen that ADHD is a mark against him. It forces him to the *defensive* position, which is ineffective. He makes excuses for his struggles rather than facing them. Glen feels tense, and he's ready to go on the attack if anything related to his difficulties gets mentioned. Doubt makes him want to *avoid* the facts, an ineffective behavior, and hide from facing the problem and getting the help he needs.

Here are some perspectives that could help Glen get off the path of self-doubt: Instead of using the ineffective behaviors of defending and avoiding, face the problem head on. Denying your ADHD won't make it go away. When you face the fact that you have real issues with distraction, focus, and organization, you can learn the skills to make sure these problems don't compromise your success. Getting available help makes you a wise problem solver. ADHD doesn't mean you're crazy, so don't pass unfair judgment on yourself and your struggles. Face your challenges. Acknowledge their existence and take the appropriate action.

When Glen replaces his give-up thoughts with go-to thoughts, here's what he comes up with:

Glen's Give-Up Thought	Glen's Go-To Thought
Everyone will think I'm some psych case.	Nobody thinks I'm a psych case but me. Lots of people talk about their ADHD, and no one seems to pass judgment on them. I'm not the only one with this diagnosis.
I don't need help.	It's hard to admit I need help, but I do. My distraction and disorganization works against me and compromises my grades, opportunities, and goals. Getting help proves I know how to deal with problems—it's a skill that will be a lifelong asset.
People will think less of me if I have this.	My mind tries to insist people will think less of me when I have no reason to think so. I know tons of kids with this issue. They're willing to put it out there, so I guess I can, too.
There's something wrong with me.	I'm not crazy or psychiatrically ill, but I do have real problems with distraction, focus, and organization. That makes me a normal kid with normal problems that are just worse for me than they are for other kids. My problems are no different than the kid who needs extra math help because his brain has trouble with spatial concepts.

CONFIDENCE PATH

Acknowledging and facing your problems means you don't let those problems define you. None of your struggles can negate your strengths. Your intellect, aptitude, and skills are as strong as anyone else's. This diagnosis doesn't change that. When you stop calling yourself nasty names and see your shortcomings as a small piece of the big picture, you're free to take the effective action of using your resources to get the help you need—whether taking medication, seeing a professional, or talking to your teachers.

CONFIDENCE MINDSET

Asking for help is a sign of self-confidence. Your ADHD does not define you. Accepting your ADHD means you can stop it from getting in your way.

⫸ *Frank's Story: My Friend Wants to Copy My Lab*

I spent five solid hours writing up my science lab. This tough assignment required major effort. I felt pride and satisfaction in my work and finished before the deadline. Then my cell rang and a friend asked me if I would share my write-up with him. I think of myself as a decent person and one to help others out, but I felt pressured and uncomfortable with this request. I think: If I say no, he'll tell everyone, and they'll think I'm a selfish loser. He'll give me a hard time if I say no. In the future he won't have my back. This may come back to haunt me.

—Frank

FRANK'S DOUBT PATH

Frank's doubt and insecurity are activated, so he's feeling pressured to do something he doesn't want to do and that he knows is wrong. In this case,

Frank's doubt-distorted expectations of being ostracized and looking bad seem valid to him. It's the doubt distortions of *extreme thinking* and *nasty name-calling* that make Frank think his friend will tell everyone and he'll be thought of as a "selfish loser." The distortion of *catastrophizing* lets Frank imagine a series of negative repercussions.

Here are some perspectives that could help Frank get off the path of self-doubt: Don't let your doubt distortions keep you from considering the true picture. An honor code violation is a serious infraction and could result in a major academic penalty. It's dangerous to *please* others at the expense of your own good and your sense of what's right. Giving over your lab does just that. Instead of letting doubt make you want to bail out your friend, have the courage to take care of yourself and your future. Effective action changes your *unassertiveness* to assertiveness. Tell your friend no, and recognize that doing what's right sometimes comes at the expense of disappointing others. In the long run, it's a small price to pay for academic integrity and a clean record.

When Frank replaces his give-up thoughts with go-to thoughts, here's what he comes up with:

Frank's Give-Up Thought	Frank's Go-To Thought
If I say no, he'll tell everyone, and they'll think I'm a selfish loser.	Most likely he won't tell anyone. It would only make him look bad to say I wouldn't let him cheat. It's possible somebody might comment, but that's a small price to pay for integrity. Saying no will not make me selfish or a loser, since every day my actions prove I'm not.
He'll give me a hard time if I say no.	Why assume he'll give me hard time? He might not. In fact, he might just say okay, no big deal. Instead of giving him the report, I could offer to help him with any sections he's stressing over. That would be real help I could give him that would let us both keep our integrity.

In the future he won't have my back.	Just because I don't give him my lab doesn't mean I will lose our friendship or that he won't look out for me in the future. In reality, I have his back by not giving him an opportunity to break the honor code and get into trouble, and by offering to help him in the way I can.
This may come back to haunt me.	The only thing that could haunt me is an infraction. I would never ask someone for work I didn't do, so this won't play against me in any way. Taking care of myself and avoiding trouble actually guarantees I'm not haunted.

CONFIDENCE PATH

Instead of worrying about pleasing your friend, think about what you value and what's important to you, and act accordingly. Have the confidence to know you are not a selfish loser, so you don't have to let someone cheat to prove otherwise.

CONFIDENCE MINDSET

Self-confidence means you don't have to please others at your own expense.

◀▮▶ *Michael's Story: I Should Leave This Party, But I Can't*

Last night, my friends and I piled into one car and drove twenty minutes to a classmate's party we found out about on Facebook. As soon as we arrived, I had a bad feeling about the scene and thought we'd get busted, but I didn't want to seem uncool by leaving. The crowd was rowdy and drunk and there were beer cans scattered everywhere. I think: If I tell my friends we should leave, they'll think I'm not cool. If I don't join in the fun, my friends won't want me along in the future. If I split, I won't be invited to go with them next time. Odds are that everything's going to be okay.

—*Michael*

MICHAEL'S DOUBT PATH

Michael's need to be included and fit in is compromising his judgment. His concern about being unwanted or negatively judged comes from his insecurity. The doubt distortion of *catastrophizing* makes Michael think that one action will lead to a pileup of negative consequences. Instead of listening to the warnings his body sends him and using good judgment to take appropriate action and leave, he lets his doubt influence him to choose *unassertiveness*, and allows the doubt distortion of *nasty name-calling* put him at risk out of fear that his friends would call him "uncool."

Here are some perspectives that could help Michael get off the path of self-doubt: Make conclusions that are relevant only to the data at hand. You can listen to your own good judgment and *assertively* talk to your friends if you don't let the fear of their opinions get in your way. Underage drinking is against the law. Whether you're drinking or not, when you're at a party where it's taking place, you risk getting arrested. Underage drinking guarantees your arrest if the party gets busted. Even one blemish on your record can close doors. Instead of worrying about reactions or future invites, have the confidence to protect yourself and speak up. If you can't persuade your friends to leave, then leave without them. You may be surprised how many were hoping someone had the sense to take the risk-free choice and leave the party.

When Michael replaces his give-up thoughts with go-to thoughts, here's what he comes up with:

Michael's Give-Up Thought	Michael's Go-To Thought
If I tell my friends we should leave, they'll think I'm not cool.	My friends might actually be grateful if I speak up. It's possible some of them want to leave too. Besides, what's more important to me, my entire future or what any given friend thinks of me? If I leave and the party gets busted, they'll think I was the smart one and wish they'd left too.
If I don't join in the fun, my friends won't want me along in the future.	With so many people here, no one will even notice what I do. No one will think twice about my disappearance. My friends like to hang out with me, so what I do on any given night is not going to change that. Lots of kids actually respect guys who choose not to drink.
If I split, I won't be invited to go with them next time.	If I get a ride home and take off, it doesn't have to be a problem. I'm making a smart decision to leave rather than stay and face potential problems. Just because I take off doesn't mean I won't be included next time.
Odds are that everything's going to be okay.	The danger is staring me in the face. Obviously drunk kids, loud music, and visible beer are an invitation for the police. No way should I ignore it. More realistically, the odds are this party is headed for disaster.

CONFIDENCE PATH

With confidence, you can recognize danger and listen to your instincts. Have the confidence not to let the need to *please* others or fear of their rejection get in your way. Taking care of yourself is a sign of maturity and says you matter. Courage to assert your opinion and make a good decision, even if it is an unpopular choice, is a positive quality that will serve you very well now and for the rest of your life. The confidence to make your own choices shows strength.

CONFIDENCE MINDSET

Self-confidence equals making your own choices regardless of what others want to do. Choosing the wise path and avoiding real danger is a sign of confidence.

⬙ *Tyler's Story: My Classmate's Dad Died and I Don't Know What to Say*

My friend and classmate's dad recently died in a tragic accident. She's been out all week and returned to school today. I really wanted to approach her and let her know how sorry I was, but I was concerned I would say the wrong thing and make her feel worse. I think: I don't want to bring it up if she doesn't want me to. I don't want to make her cry. I don't want to say the wrong thing. Maybe before class isn't the right time.

—Tyler

TYLER'S DOUBT PATH

Providing condolence and support for a person who has suffered a significant loss is tough for everyone. Textbooks don't explain what to say and when to say it. It's normal for Tyler to feel insecure in this situation. When Tyler imagines his behavior will have a negative effect on his friend, he's allowing the doubt distortion of *forecasting the future* to take over. The ineffective behavior of *worrying* stirs nagging thoughts about how his friend will react and stops Tyler from approaching her.

Here are some perspectives that could help Tyler get off the path of self-doubt: *Look at it from different angles* and recognize that there's no such thing as a perfect way to provide support and sympathy to someone who's experienced tragic loss. Your doubt distortion of *expecting too much* and your ineffective behavior of *perfectionism* block you from being genuine and naturally compassionate. Doubt leads you to believe there's only one right thing to say and one perfect time to say it. In reality, there's never just one right thing or perfect time. Mentioning her loss shows you care and you're thinking about her. When you provide support and comfort, she knows her friends are there for her. Think how much you'd value your friends' support if you were facing a rough time.

When Tyler replaces his give-up thoughts with go-to thoughts, here's what he comes up with:

Tyler's Give-Up Thought	Tyler's Go-To Thought
I don't want to bring it up if she doesn't want me to.	Showing someone I care can never be a mistake.
I don't want to make her cry.	She might cry, but that doesn't mean I shouldn't say anything. Her tears just mean she has strong feelings. There's also the chance she won't cry. Either way, she'll probably be grateful I acknowledged her loss. I can't let my fear of her reaction stop me from telling her I'm genuinely concerned.
I don't want to say the wrong thing.	There's no one right thing to say. It's not the words that matter, it's the support and comfort I provide by acknowledging her loss.
Maybe before class isn't the right time.	There's no perfect time, so don't delay. When I let her know right away that I'm here as a support, I give her the message that I care.

CONFIDENCE PATH

Just because you feel uncomfortable doesn't mean you can't approach your friend. Talk back to the doubt distortion of *depending only on your emotions*. Don't let your insecure feelings keep you from being a supportive friend. Let your friend know you care. Have the self-confidence to recognize that her reaction or emotions aren't signs that you messed up. Accept there is no perfect approach and let your friend know you want to be there for her.

CONFIDENCE MINDSET

Supporting your friends during difficult times means you put yourself out there for them even if it makes you uncomfortable. Face your discomfort, knowing it will pass.

The Bottom Line

You are your own greatest resource when dealing with tough stuff. Having self-confidence means that when push comes to shove, you know you can handle whatever develops. It's time to treat and talk to yourself the same way you treat and talk to others. Be your own personal coach, friend, or cheerleader rather than critic, bully, or pessimist. View the tough stuff in objective ways, and work to take the personal meanings out of the equation. Stick to the facts and you'll never lose your way. Be realistic about how much control you do or don't have in situations. Recognize that your internal and external resources will guide you. Encourage yourself to find meaning from upset so you continue to stretch, learn, and grow as a self-confident person.

CHAPTER 8

Building Unshakable Self-Confidence

"If you don't believe in yourself,
then who will believe in you?"

—*Michael Korda (author)*

You have the power to be confident because it comes from within you. When you see life through a clear and accurate lens, believe in yourself, and at your core see yourself in a positive way, you're self-confident. It's all about the way you think. Growing your self-confidence is a process, and you learn from experience. Let's find out where you stand.

QUIZ: Test Your Confidence

Read each of the following sentences. If you agree with a sentence, give yourself a 3. If you disagree, write down a 1. If you're somewhere in the middle, give yourself a 2.

_____ I can start a conversation with anyone in any situation at any time.

_____ I am willing to tackle almost any task presented to me.

_____ I am at ease with who I am.

_____ I can ask for help if I need it.

_____ I take it for granted that people want to spend time with me.

_____ I'm comfortable operating at my own pace.

_____ I can do the things I like even if I do them alone.

_____ I am willing to face challenging situations head on.

_____ I am comfortable giving my honest opinion.

_____ I don't get rattled when I make a mistake.

Add up your score: _____

What does your score mean?

28–30 You are super-confident.

25–27 You are confident.

16–24 You are somewhat lacking in confidence.

10–15 You are seriously lacking in confidence.

If you scored 25 or higher, you're confident. You have the self-confidence to face nearly any situation, knowing you can handle it. Your confidence enables you to reach for your goals, try new things, act independently and effectively, and enter social situations free from doubt.

When you believe you're competent and a good, likeable person, you become your own greatest resource. Confidence helps you highlight your strengths. It also enables you to recognize and identify your weaknesses so that you can improve these areas, using outside resources if necessary. You've gained unshakable self-esteem because you hold a good opinion of yourself. You recognize that situations may temporarily be distressing but do not allow it to change your core view of who you are.

If you scored below 25, you need to keep building your self-confidence. Reinforcing your skills will get you there. Retraining your brain to move from self-doubt to confidence is no different than strengthening a muscle through weight training: you build up to more reps, or to more weight, over repeated workouts.

Being confident is a choice. It's up to you to build confidence by taking control of how you think. Remember: how you interpret a situation influences your feelings and actions. Changing your doubt-based thoughts is the key to changing how you feel about yourself and your behavior. Confidence enables you to see the accurate picture.

Now it's your turn to try out the methods you learned throughout this book. Use the following series of exercises as often as you need to as you encounter tough choices and work to strengthen your self-confidence. Writing down the particulars of a difficult situation can help you capture your give-up thoughts and use the facts to replace them with go-to thoughts.

Confidence Mindset-Building Exercises

The next few pages consist of a number of exercises to help you systematically build your confidence mindset. Work through these exercises whenever you're dealing with a particularly troublesome situation.

EXERCISE: Thought Capturing

Start here by describing a situation that's causing you distress, using more paper if you need to.

_____

_____

_____

_____

Now think about that specific situation and write down all the thoughts that pop into your head. Use more paper if you need to, and keep going until you run out of thoughts. Don't judge them yet—just get them down.

_____

_____

_____

_____

Look at the thoughts you wrote down in the above exercise. Are they give-up thoughts, or go-to thoughts? Hint: Are your thoughts negatively biased, inaccurate interpretations of reality driven by doubt distortions (see chapter 2) or are they accurate, fact-based, unbiased perceptions? Keep in mind that a thought can be a fact, but when we blow it out of proportion or draw faulty conclusions from it, it turns into a give-up thought. When we accept a straightforward fact and don't judge it, it becomes a source of information that can be used as a go-to thought. Go-to thoughts help us to see the situation accurately even when we have very strong feelings about it. The next few exercises will help you determine which of your thoughts are based on doubt.

Is It a Give-Up Thought?

Give-up thoughts typically stir up strong negative feelings. Paying attention to your emotional and physiological signals can provide clues to the presence of powerful give-up thoughts.

Warning Signs of a Give-Up Thought	No	Yes
The thought is particularly negative.		
The thought is packed with fearful concerns.		
Thinking the thought makes me experience strong unpleasant feelings like anger, fear, sadness, guilt, or shame.		
When I hold the thought in my mind, I experience disagreeable bodily symptoms or sensations such as shaking, tremors, flushing, sweating, clamminess, shallow breathing, or pain.		

EXERCISE: Did You Use Effective Thinking?

Now that you have captured your thoughts about a given situation, you can begin to determine if your thinking is clear and unbiased. This checklist and the lists that follow will help you gather information and clarify your thinking about each of the thoughts you've captured. Then you will have the opportunity to take each give-up thought and use your information and analysis to convert it to a go-to thought.

For each of the thoughts you wrote down, ask yourself: "When I was coming up with this thought, did I use any of these effective thinking strategies?"

Effective Thinking Strategy	No	Yes
I got information from more than one source.		
I didn't jump to conclusions.		
I considered all the possibilities.		
I looked at it from different angles.		
I asked myself if this is one unique situation or a pattern.		
I made conclusions that were relevant only to the data at hand.		
I considered my past experiences.		

If you were able to answer yes to one or more of these questions, you have already done some effective thinking about the situation. Applying all these strategies to your most troublesome give-up thoughts will help you move them toward go-to thoughts.

EXERCISE: Did You Use Ineffective Thinking?

The following questions will help you identify possible errors in your thinking.

1. Looking at the evidence, are the thoughts you've identified as give-up thoughts based on facts and accurate, or are they inaccurate with no evidence to support them?

   _____

   _____

2. Are there other possible explanations? What are they?

   _____

   _____

3. What is the worst that could happen, and what are the chances that it will actually happen?

    _____

    _____

4. Would I be able to cope if the worst thing did happen?

    _____

    _____

5. What is the best possible outcome?

    _____

    _____

6. What is the most likely outcome? How different is it from my worst fears?

    _____

    _____

7. What would I say to a friend who had these same, doubtful give-up thoughts? What would a good friend say to me?

    _____

    _____

8. Overall, what is a more reasonable way to see this situation?

    _____

    _____

EXERCISE: Did You Use Doubt Distortions?

Were there any doubt distortions in your thinking? Check off all of the doubt distortions you found in your give-up thoughts. Remember: doubt distortions are thinking errors that filter your thinking in a negative way (see chapter 2 for a full discussion of all these distortions).

I See This Doubt Distortion in My Thinking	No	Yes
Extreme thinking: Seeing myself in terms of all or nothing rather than looking at the big picture.		
Depending only on my emotions: Letting my emotions reign and ignoring the facts of the situation, or assuming I know the facts when none yet exist.		
Nasty name-calling: Labeling myself in a negative way.		
Catastrophizing: Taking a small, possibly unimportant situation and making it bigger, or more likely; expecting the worst consequences.		
Forecasting the future: Imagining my future in the most negative or fearful way.		
Expecting too much: Operating on imperatives. The words *must, should*, and *have to* lead to unrelenting expectations.		
Zooming in on the negative: Not seeing the big picture and focusing exclusively on the negatives.		

EXERCISE: Replacing Give-Up Thoughts with Go-To Thoughts

It's time to systematically replace your give-up thoughts with go-to thoughts. By carefully examining your thoughts and identifying your doubt distortions, you will see accurate, realistic go-to thoughts emerging. Doubt drives your give-up thoughts, but confident go-to thoughts counter them and defeat your doubt.

Go back to your original list of every thought you had about this situation, and transfer all the thoughts you identified as give-up thoughts to the left-hand column below. Using the analysis you've already done in the last few exercises, create your alternative go-to thoughts. Write these in the right-hand column opposite the give-up thoughts they replace. Use additional paper if you need to.

Give-Up Thought	Go-To Thought

EXERCISE: Did Your Give-Up Thoughts Lead to Ineffective Behavior?

Now think about this situation from the perspective of the actions you've taken—or actions you feel compelled to take based on your give-up thoughts. Did your give-up thoughts lead you to think about or take one or more ineffective-behavior actions? Remember that even effective-behavior actions can become ineffective ones when you overuse them rigidly or repetitively, or in situations where they're just not the appropriate action.

Use the checklist below to identify ineffective behavioral strategies you tried, or wanted to try, when dealing with this particular situation.

I Tried (or Wanted to Try) This Behavioral Strategy	No	Yes
Avoiding: I wouldn't face up to things, I dodged, or I didn't deal.		
Quitting: I gave up.		
Distracting: I focused on other things rather than on the priority.		
Seeking perfection: I concentrated on getting things exactly right.		
Seeking control: I tried to take charge of everyone and everything.		
Pleasing: I sought to make everyone else happy without considering myself.		
Worrying: I made up (and obsessed on) nagging thoughts about what might happen.		
Being unassertive: I stayed passive rather than directly asserting myself or communicating directly and honestly.		
Manipulating: I manipulated others to do or act by twisting the facts or maneuvering things in a self-serving way.		
Defending: I made excuses or went on the attack.		

Replacing Ineffective Behaviors with Effective Ones

Ask yourself if these behavioral strategies were helpful or not in the situation. Recognize that when the strategy you are using is ineffective, it's time to try an alternative. Consider using one or more of the effective action options below in the future.

Effective Action Options to Replace Avoidance Behaviors (Avoiding, Quitting, Distracting)

- **Problem solve:** Define the problem, consider your options, weigh the pros and cons, and pick a solution.

- **Prioritize:** Don't let unimportant distractions get in the way of taking care of more urgent items.

- **Stop the delay tactics:** No more excuses or distractions. Keep on the task.

- **Schedule in timed breaks:** No impulsive interruptions for snacks or drinks. Plan your break times.

- **Take action:** Make a plan and put it on your schedule. Tackle it head-on. Action can happen even if you don't feel like it or don't want to. Start doing.

- **Take small steps:** Break the overall goal into smaller manageable tasks.

- **Just try:** Give it your best effort and make an attempt.

- **Keep it simple:** Be clear about the task, and don't make it more complicated than it is.

- **Use help:** Try it on your own first, but use your resources if you need additional information or assistance.

- **Give yourself credit:** Each thing you do counts.

- **Do it without knowing the result:** Don't let fear and anxiety about the unknown stop you before you even begin.

- **Stay focused and present:** Stay on task and focus 100 percent of your attention. It's not the time to check Facebook, text friends, or glance at TV.

- **Follow through:** Hang in there and see the task through until it's done.

Effective Action Options to Replace Perfectionist Behaviors (Seeking Perfection or Control, Pleasing, Worrying)

- **Develop realistic standards:** Accept that good enough really is good enough.

- **Make a choice:** Use the information you have to make the most reasonable decision and accept there is no perfect decision.

- **Yield:** Take control some of the time but not all of the time.

- **Take a team approach:** Let others participate and share the responsibility.

- **Give up the need to always please:** Consider your needs and feelings as part of the equation.

- **Be logical:** Don't take care of others at the expense of your well-being.

- **Turn off your worry:** Focus on the facts.

- **Stay present:** Know that worry doesn't keep you safe or change the outcome.

- Think in the "for-now" and not in the "for-ever."

Effective Action Options to Replace Ineffective Communication Behaviors (Being Unassertive, Manipulating, Defending)

- **State the facts:** If someone's done something or said something that bothers you or puts you in a compromising situation, be prepared to tell them exactly what they said or did.

- **Speak up:** Ask for what you want, or let others know what action you plan to take. Be clear and specific.

- **Listen to others:** Acknowledging what others think, feel, or want makes them more willing to compromise.

- **Compromise:** Consider your best interest and the interest of others when finding a solution. Be willing to be flexible.

- **Be assertive:** Say what you mean and mean what you say.

- **Present the full picture:** Be accurate and straightforward.

- **Give equal weight to information:** Don't exaggerate to make a point.

- **See both sides:** The truth is usually somewhere in between.

- **Take responsibility:** Instead of making excuses, acknowledge your role.

- **Be objective:** Consider the facts before you react.

- **Don't blow up:** Keep your cool so you can effectively deliver your message.

EXERCISE: What's Your Confidence Path?

Now that you're equipped with the truth about a particular situation that troubles you, write down your confidence path. Your confidence path is your objective understanding of the situation. It's the conclusion you draw from your fact-based, go-to thoughts. You can think of it as the voice of a wise coach, kind friend, greatest fan, or other person who believes in you. What would that person advise you about how to think of this troublesome situation? How would that person advise you to act? For example: set realistic goals; review your options; come up with a plan of action; be realistic; recognize and give yourself credit for your strengths; develop realistic standards for yourself; stay in the present; don't beat yourself up; assert yourself. Add the specifics of your particular situation; for example: "Remember Mom can't help if she doesn't know all the facts," or "You don't need to base your actions on your friend's opinion."

_____

_____

_____

_____

_____

_____

EXERCISE: What's Your Confidence Mindset?

Use what you have learned in this specific example to write down your confidence mindset: a positive, accurate, and realistic message to yourself. You can use this message as your guide to maintain unshakable confidence. Your confidence mindset is like the voice in your head that brings out your very best, equipping you to face the demands of achievement and your social life.

Here are some phrases you might use in creating a confidence mindset: _I have the confidence to use my own judgment; I'm good just the way I am; I don't have to be perfect to be a success; I am a complex package and not defined by any given shortcoming; I can focus on the doing and not on the outcome; rejection is not a global statement about me; if I like myself then others will like me, too; trying my best_ *is the key; taking social risks means I have a chance of getting what I want; doing things that are hard for me means I will have the opportunity to grow.*

_____

_____

_____

_____

_____

_____

Continue to Build Your Self-Confidence

Self-confidence is like a plant: it needs to be fertilized and fed in order to take root and grow. Make nurturing your self-confidence a part of your daily life, and all of life's ups and downs will become less of a challenge and more of an opportunity. Here are some tips to keep you on the path of growing, thriving self-confidence.

Assess

- Take the Test Your Confidence quiz (at the beginning of this chapter) every few weeks to see how you're doing.

- Think of sadness, anxiety, upset, and other emotions as guides signaling you to stop and look at your thinking.

- Look out for times when you overreact emotionally, physically, or mentally: these are also times to slow down and examine your thinking.

◆ Pay attention to your self-criticism or personal, self-doubting insults. They signal the presence of doubt-driven thinking.

Repair

◆ Stay alert: keep examining your thinking so you can check it out with the facts.

◆ Work to differentiate doubt from realistic concern.

◆ Use the Confidence Mindset-Building exercises (this chapter) in your daily life to strengthen your confidence muscle and build your unshakable self-esteem.

◆ Remember not to be afraid of negative feelings. Without them you wouldn't enjoy the positives as much.

◆ Don't be afraid of your bodily sensations: they are just warning signals telling you to pay attention or be prepared.

◆ Strive to live without fear of others' judgments.

◆ Recognize that you can handle any situation, either on your own or using your outside resources.

Grow

◆ See yourself in the most positive, realistic, and accurate way possible.

◆ Count on yourself first.

◆ Know you can manage stress.

◆ Reach for your full potential.

◆ Run daily experiments with yourself by trying something new or doing a familiar thing differently.

Maintain

- Enjoy the feeling of happiness and success whenever it comes.

- Journal, text, or e-mail yourself the good stuff in your life on a daily basis. Try to come up with at least five things per day.

- Set daily, weekly, monthly, or yearly goals for yourself so you can dream and put trying into action.

- Update your own confidence status on a regular basis by adding new or improved internal and external assets and resources.

- Define yourself using all the positive assets, qualities, strengths, skills, features, and roles that come to mind. For example, I'm a good person, smart, attractive, caring, a good listener, a conscientious student, a nice sister, a loving child, a respectable athlete who knows how to work hard and is driven and motivated.

- Use compliments and positive feedback from others to add to your confidence mindset.

- When good things happen, give yourself credit for the role you played.

The Bottom Line

Building, growing, and maintaining self-confidence is essential to success and happiness. Self-confidence is something everyone can achieve. You do it by looking objectively at the situations you face and focusing on the facts. This allows you to capture and defeat the thoughts you have that are inaccurate and biased. Now that you have learned how to capture and analyze your thoughts, you can more objectively evaluate your thinking and see how doubt can cloud your self-view and world-view. Over time and with practice, you can defeat doubt, and a new, accurate, self-confident view of yourself will grow. Remember, sometimes your thoughts are true, and can alert you to be realistically concerned. By using the skills you have learned in this book, you can more immediately differentiate realistic concern from doubt so you can choose the appropriate, effective action. By continuing to assess, repair, grow, and maintain your self-confidence, you can build unshakable self-esteem, leave doubt and fear behind, and live up to your fullest potential for success and happiness.

Marci G. Fox, PhD, is a licensed psychologist, expert in cognitive therapy, internationally recognized speaker, and coauthor of *Think Confident, Be Confident*. She is an adjunct faculty member at the Beck Institute for Cognitive Behavior Therapy and a founding fellow in the Academy of Cognitive Therapy who also serves on its board of examiners. Her private practice is in Boca Raton, FL.

Leslie Sokol, PhD, is a licensed psychologist, expert in cognitive therapy, acclaimed national and international speaker, and coauthor of *Think Confident, Be Confident*. She is a senior faculty member and past director of education at the Beck Institute for Cognitive Behavior Therapy and distinguished founding fellow, past president, and credentials chair of the Academy of Cognitive Therapy. Her private practice is in the Philadelphia suburbs.

www.thinkconfidentbeconfident.com
www.cbtexperts.com

Foreword writer **Aaron T. Beck, MD**, is President Emeritus and founder of the Beck Institute for Cognitive Behavior, University Professor Emeritus at the University of Pennsylvania, and honorary president of the Academy of Cognitive Therapy.

Foreword writer **Judith S. Beck, PhD**, is president of the Beck Institute for Cognitive Behavior Therapy and clinical associate professor of psychology in psychiatry at the University of Pennsylvania.